FINDING
GOD

AFTER GOD's OWN HEART

James Gross

Finding GOD After GOD's Own Heart
Library of Congress Publication Data
American Revision Committee, *The Holy Bible,* American Standard Version is used for scripture quotes
Life.Church for YouVersion Bible App is used for *The Holy Bible* text.
Gross, James.

Finding GOD After GOD's Own Heart / James Gross
ISBN 978-0692843901
ISBN (e-book) 978-0-9987054-0-8

Finding GOD: After GOD's Own Heart is a work based in the author's opinion, experiences, and interpretation. Where real people, events, establishments, organizations, or locales appear, they are nonfiction.

To my family, Deana Gross, Bridgette Gross,
Joshua Gross, Shelby Gross,
Caleb Gross, and Isaiah Gross.
Nathanial "Dad" Wheat, Kim Wheat,
Mary Clay, and Christopher Wheat

Acknowledgments

The people of the Life.Church: YouVersion Bible App, who liberally gives GOD's WORD, sharing the gospel with the hungry and thirsty. All scripture references are from the American Standard Version of *The Holy Bible* translated by the American Revision Committee.

This book started as a letter to my son, Joshua. I felt like our relationship was breached, so I asked GOD to build a bridge to my son. GOD told me that I had an advantage because children naturally love their father, so I had to reach out. I wanted my son to know how my thought process works. Basically, what makes me, me. Of course, that was inspired by GOD, WHO provides HIS WORD in order for me to understand HIM. Once I started typing, it poured out.

The man I call Dad displayed humility that I have yet to see duplicated among people. My Mom and I were having a conversation about my Dad, and I reminded her of how he would bring us together as a family. He would sit at the head of the table, and listen to everyone's stories with a delight-filled face. He never said much, but he was a joy to be around.

My Dad came to see me, when I had closed my small business. Even though I had my family with me, I was in a low and lonely place. My Dad took me outside alone, and I remember him saying I had to snap out of it, but my mind was caught up on a clear, starry night sky.

I thought of the prayers GOD had answered for me, and the multitude of stars HE had to align for me to be living. That is when I knew, I have to be completely depend on HIM. No more gorging, then lounging, it was time for a steady diet of the WORD.

Finding GOD
After GOD's Own Heart

Table of Contents

INTROSPECTION

Chapter 1

When seeking GOD, I must come to terms with both my lack of sovereignty, and the unction to remit from my sinful nature. Which is the compelling power of the HOLY SPIRIT working to overcome the sin that is at work within me. Seeking GOD coerced by a zealous sense of duty and ambition is like giving sugar to a child. Reasonable adults know the results will most likely be harmful, but still cannot see its finality.

Emotionally charged random scripture reading can easily make me overzealous with an unbalanced idea of judgment, but this cocktail sensationalizes raw emotions that are neither quickly nor easily subdued. It is an impulse like getting a vehicle I cannot afford, or saying something horrible to a loved one that I cannot retract.

Seeking GOD is meant to be slow and reflective. It is a walk not a run. If I am rushing to find GOD, then I am amiss. I am to be mindful that in all the facets of seeking GOD, my perception is always the reason I cannot find GOD. If I seek GOD to find significance in life, then pride subtly manipulates my thoughts of my importance to GOD's kingdom.

Pride persuades me that if I am in charge, things run more efficiently and lives are enjoyable. Pride coherences me to value myself above all others except for GOD of course, but in due course my pride will rescind that exception. Pride is a usurper of all that is good, and therefore I must cast it down by the knowledge of GOD who reigns eternal.

My method for seeking GOD is praying before reading a chapter of *The Holy Bible* at night and one in the morning from beginning to end through a specific book at that time, but I neither try to memorize chapter nor verse number, only content. Chapters and verses were added to *The Holy Bible* for convenience, but I need to understand its principles. I try to keep each chapter to at least ten verses mainly because *Psalms* has short chapters. I think of it like a meal, so I neither want to gorge, nor malnourish my spirit, and sometimes I will study different subjects, but that does not substitute my daily reading.

A

Deuteronomy 17:14-20, "When thou art come unto the land which JEHOVAH thy GOD giveth thee, and shalt possess it, and shalt dwell therein, and shalt say, I will set a king over me, like all the nations that are round about me; thou shalt surely set him king over thee, whom JEHOVAH thy GOD shall choose: one from among thy brethren shalt thou set king over thee; thou mayest not put a foreigner over thee, who is not thy brother. Only he shall not multiply horses to himself, nor cause the people to return to Egypt, to the end that he may multiply horses; forasmuch as JEHOVAH hath said unto you, Ye shall henceforth return no more that way. Neither shall he multiply wives to himself, that his heart turn not away: neither shall he greatly multiply to himself silver and gold. **And it shall be, when he sitteth upon the throne of his kingdom, that he shall write him a copy of this law in a book, out of and it shall be with him, and he shall read therein all the days of his life**; that he may learn to fear JEHOVAH his GOD, to keep all the words of this law and these statutes, to do them; that his heart be not lifted up above his brethren, and that he turn not aside from the commandment, to the right hand, or to the left: to the end that he may prolong his days in his kingdom, he and his children, in the midst of Israel."

Ω

Most daily praying and reading takes about fifteen minutes, but over a lifetime it adds up. *The Holy Bible* has 1,189 chapters, so approximately every two years it is read in its entirety. My understanding of seeking GOD connects Moses' words of the duty of a king to the Paul's words of being a joint-heir of the KING of kings.

A

2

Romans 8:14-17, "For as many as are led by the SPIRIT of GOD, these are sons of GOD. For ye received not the spirit of bondage again unto fear; but ye received the spirit of adoption, whereby we cry, ABBA, FATHER. The SPIRIT HIMSELF beareth witness with our spirit, that we are children of GOD: and if children, then heirs; heirs of GOD, and joint-heirs with CHRIST; if so be that we suffer with HIM, that we may be also glorified with HIM."

Ω

GOD views me as a joint-heir with CHRIST the KING, and therefore my regal standing in HIM is subjugated to HIS prescription of the royal obligation. My goal is to find HIM, but goals always have obstacles. Pride, ambition, hurt, impatience, ignorance, intolerance, prejudice, slothfulness, indifference, and ambivalence are lens of some reasons I do not see GOD in situations.

Not to say that I am above all these issues, but being aware of their presence allows me to adjust my focus on HIM as if tweaking HIS visibility through a microscope. If uncertain...wait, investigate, research, check references, ask questions, document evidence, and then wait again. In the meantime, live the simple life GOD has instructed me.

A

Ephesians 5:21-6:9, "subjecting yourselves one to another in the fear of CHRIST. Wives, be in subjection unto your own husbands, as unto the LORD. For the husband is the head of the wife, as CHRIST also is the HEAD of the church, being HIMSELF the SAVIOR of the body. But as the church is subject to CHRIST, so let the wives also be to their husbands in everything. Husbands, love your wives, even as CHRIST also loved the church, and gave HIMSELF up for it; that HE might sanctify it, having cleansed it by the washing of water with the WORD, that HE might present the church to HIMSELF a glorious church, not having spot or wrinkle or any such thing; but that it should be holy and without blemish. Even so ought husbands also to love their own wives as their own bodies. He that loveth his own wife loveth himself: for no man ever hated his own flesh; but nourisheth and cherisheth it, even as CHRIST also the church; because we are members of HIS body. For this cause shall a man leave his father and mother, and shall cleave to his wife; and the two shall become one flesh. This mystery is great: but I speak in regard of CHRIST and of the church. Nevertheless do ye also severally love each one his own wife even as himself; and let the wife see that she fear her husband. Children, obey your parents in the LORD: for this is right. Honor thy father and mother (which is the first commandment with promise), that it may be well with thee, and thou mayest live long on the earth. And, ye fathers, provoke not your children to wrath: but nurture them in the chastening and admonition of the LORD. Servants, be obedient unto them that according to the flesh are your masters, with fear and trembling, in singleness of your heart, as unto CHRIST; not in the way of eyeservice, as men-pleasers; but as servants of CHRIST, doing the will of GOD from the heart; with good will doing service, as unto the LORD, and not unto men: knowing that whatsoever good thing each one doeth, the same shall he receive again from the LORD, whether he be bond or free. And, ye masters, do the same things unto them, and forbear threatening: knowing that HE who is both their MASTER and yours is in heaven, and there is no respect of persons with HIM."

1 Timothy 5:8, "But if any provideth not for his own, and specially his own household, he hath denied the faith, and is worse than an unbeliever."

Ω

The latter verse is derived from scripture referring to widows, but it delves into the deeper subject matter of my responsibility to my family. Paul writes about me taking care of my house, and how that is irrevocably linked to my faith. If I am not maintaining the necessities of those in my household, then I have forfeited all the promises

4

of GOD because that position is in worse standing with GOD than the unbelievers HE kept out of "The Promise Land." I have to submit to this government's laws, and my employer to secure my family's needs. In order to find GOD, I have to willfully submit to authority like JESUS yielded to Pilate.

A

John 19:10-11, "Pilate therefore saith unto HIM (JESUS), Speakest THOU not unto me? Knowest THOU not that I have power to release THEE, and have power to crucify THEE? JESUS answered him, Thou wouldest have no power against ME, except it were given thee from above: therefore he that delivered ME unto thee hath greater sin."

Ω

My current position in life dictates the level of authority GOD has placed me. I must know my position as David had insight into his position's limitations. King Saul had pursued David in attempts to take his life, and David had opportunities to slay Saul, but refused to harm him.

A

1 Samuel 24:4-7, "And the men of David said unto him, Behold, the day of which JEHOVAH said unto thee, Behold, I will deliver thine enemy into thy hand, and thou shalt do to him as it shall seem good unto thee. Then David arose, and cut off the skirt of Saul's robe privily. And it came to pass afterward, that David's heart smote him, because he had cut off Saul's skirt. And he said unto his men, JEHOVAH forbid that I should do this thing unto my lord, JEHOVAH's anointed, to put forth my hand against him, seeing he is JEHOVAH's anointed. So David checked his men with these words, and suffered them not to rise against Saul. And Saul rose up out of the cave, and went on his way."

1 Samuel 26:9-11, "And David said to Abishai, Destroy him not; for who can put forth his hand against JEHOVAH's anointed, and be guiltless? And David said, As JEHOVAH liveth, JEHOVAH will smite him; or his day shall come to die; or he shall go down into battle and perish. JEHOVAH forbid that I should put forth my hand against JEHOVAH's anointed: but now take, I pray thee, the spear that is at his head, and the cruse of water, and let us go."

Ω

David had already been anointed by Samuel to replace King Saul, but had not ascended to the position of king yet (detailed in Chapter Four: Patience). He had a clear understanding of his position, and his resolve of inaction is an example of practical application from scriptures he knew. David's understanding was from the practical application of scripture from *Genesis* and *Exodus*.

A

Genesis 20:1-7, "And Abraham journeyed from thence toward the land of the South, and dwelt between Kadesh and Shur. And he sojourned in Gerar. And Abraham said of Sarah his wife, She is my sister. And Abimelech king of Gerar sent, and took Sarah. But GOD came to Abimelech in a dream of the night, and said to him, Behold, thou art but a dead man, because of the woman whom thou hast taken. For she is a man's wife. Now Abimelech had not come near her. And he said, LORD, wilt THOU slay even a righteous nation? Said he not himself unto me, She is my sister? And she, even she herself said, He is my brother. In the integrity of my heart and the innocency of my hands have I done this. And GOD said unto him in the dream, Yea, I know that in the integrity of thy heart thou has done this, and I also withheld thee from sinning against ME. Therefore suffered I thee not to touch her. Now therefore restore the man's wife. For he is a prophet, and he shall pray for thee, and thou shalt live. And if thou restore her not, know thou that thou shalt surely die, thou, and all that are thine."

Exodus 22:28, "Thou shalt not revile GOD, nor curse a ruler of thy people."

Ω

The concept of being respectful of authority is still applicable today. GOD allows moral and immoral people in positions of authority. In either case, I do not have the authority to do contrary from my instructions. Paul understood the precept of position as well.

A

Acts 23:1-5, "And Paul, looking stedfastly on the council, said, Brethren, I have lived before GOD in all good conscience until this day. And the high priest Ananias commanded them that stood by him to smite him on the mouth. Then said Paul unto him, GOD shall smite thee, thou whited wall: and sittest thou to judge me according to the law, and commandest me to be smitten contrary to the law? And they that stood by said, Revilest thou GOD's high priest? And Paul said, I knew not, brethren, that he was high priest: for it is written, Thou shalt not speak evil of a ruler of thy people."

Ω

Sometimes the line of authority gets blurred because collectively all are governed by a system of laws, and individuals may overstep their rights. I am entitled to certain rights by law, so at times I have to come to terms with the limitations of my rights because of my position. As an example, I have free speech, and I may be good at my job, but my boss has a right to tell me to do my job differently.

I do not have a right to tell him how to do his differently. Honesty and truth are essential for a true evaluation to understand myself in order to find GOD.

SEEK

Chapter 2

What does it mean to seek GOD? Is GOD lost, or has GOD forgotten where HE started, or where HE is going? First, I must understand the question has absolutely nothing to do with GOD's identity, but my own lack of bearing and identity. If I am lost, then in order to find GOD I need directions, and a guide. Now anyone using GPS (Global Positioning System) or a map knows how confusing either can be, but a good guide makes the path seem clear and simple. GPS or my map is *The Holy Bible,* and the good guide is GOD's indwelling SPIRIT, known as the HOLY SPIRIT.

A

John 14:26, (JESUS speaking) "But the COMFORTER, which is the HOLY GHOST, whom the FATHER will send in MY name, HE shall teach you all things, and bring all things to your remembrance, whatsoever I have said unto you."

1 John 2:27, "And as for you, the anointing which ye received of HIM abideth in you, and ye need not that any one teach you; but as HIS anointing teacheth you; concerning all things, and is true, and is no lie, and even as it taught you, ye abide in HIM."

Ω

By prophets GOD informed the children of Israel of their necessity of the HOLY SPIRIT. The children of Israel had an outlook of futuristic fulfillment instead of understanding the proximity of their dire spiritual crisis. Notice this message from *The Old Testament* is still applicable today.

A

Jeremiah 31:33-34, "But this is the covenant that I will make with the house of Israel after those days, saith JEHOVAH: I will put MY law in their inward parts, and in their heart will I write it; and I will be their GOD, and they shall be MY people: and they shall teach no more every man his neighbor, and every man his brother, saying, Know JEHOVAH; for they shall all know ME, from the least of them unto the greatest of them, saith JEHOVAH: for I will forgive their iniquity, and their sin will I remember no more."

Ezekiel 36:23-28, "And I will sanctify MY great name, which hath been profaned among the nations, which ye have profaned in the midst of them; and the nations shall know that I am JEHOVAH, saith the LORD JEHOVAH, when I shall be sanctified in you before their eyes. For I will take you from among the nations, and gather you out of all the countries, and will bring you into your own land. And I will sprinkle clean water upon you, and ye shall be clean: from all your filthiness, and from all your idols, will I cleanse you. A new heart also will I give you, and a new spirit will I put within you; and I will take away the stony heart out of your flesh, and I will give you a heart of flesh. And I will put MY SPIRIT within you, and cause you to walk in MY statutes, and ye shall keep MINE ordinances, and do them. And ye shall dwell in the land that I gave to your fathers; and ye shall be MY people, and I will be your GOD."

Ω

The HOLY SPIRIT I have is personalized and acclimated to me, so GOD and I have a distinct, direct relationship from everyone else. When I choose to engage in more scripture, I am feeding the HOLY SPIRIT in me. Contrarily, if I choose less scripture, he starves, and spiritual starvation leads to carnal decisions. Unlike JESUS, who received an unlimited supply of the HOLY SPIRIT, the HOLY SPIRIT in me is limited. It is imperative for me to feed my measure of faith of the HOLY SPIRIT.

John 3:34-36, "For HE (JESUS) whom GOD hath sent speaketh the words of GOD: for HE giveth not the SPIRIT by measure. The FATHER loveth the SON, and hath given all things into HIS hand. He that believeth on the SON hath eternal life; but he that obeyeth not the SON shall not see life, but the wrath of GOD abideth on him."

Romans 12:3, "For I say, through the grace that was given me, to every man that is among you, not to think of himself more highly than he ought to think; but to think as to think soberly, according as GOD hath dealt to each man a measure of faith."

Ephesians 4:7, "But unto each one of us was the grace given according to the measure of the gift of CHRIST."

Ω

The measure of the HOLY SPIRIT GOD gives differs on an individual basis, but I am to learn what HIS expectation is for me to empower my spiritual progress. Now hearing, seeing, knowing, and understanding scripture are very different things. I can hear without seeing, see without knowing, and know without understanding, but I cannot understand without either hearing, seeing, or knowing. Under GOD's instruction, understanding is not a prerequisite for obedience, but obedience is mandatory.

A

Isaiah 6:8-10, "And I heard the voice of the LORD, saying, Whom shall I send, and who will go for US? Then I said, Here am I; send me. And HE said, Go, and tell this people, Hear ye indeed, but understand not; and see ye indeed, but perceive not. Make the heart of this people fat, and make their ears heavy, and shut their eyes; lest they see with their eyes, and hear with their ears, and understand with their heart, and turn again, and be healed."

Matthew 13:11-15, "And HE (JESUS) answered and said unto them, Unto you it is given to know the mysteries of the kingdom of heaven, but to them it is not given. For whosoever hath, to him shall be given, and he shall have abundance: but whosoever hath not, from him shall be taken away even that which he hath. Therefore speak I to them in parables; because seeing they see not, and hearing they hear not, neither do they understand."

1 Samuel 15:22-23, "And Samuel said, Hath JEHOVAH as great delight in burnt-offerings and sacrifices, as in obeying the voice of JEHOVAH? Behold, to obey is better than sacrifice, and to hearken than the fat of rams. For rebellion is as the sin of witchcraft, and stubbornness is as idolatry and teraphim. Because thou hast rejected the word of JEHOVAH, he hath also rejected thee from being king."

Ω

My salvation is in the WORD of GOD, and trusting HIS WORD and the power of the HOLY SPIRIT is requisite to accomplish the desire of HIS plan for me. My will has to be trained to yield in obedience to HIS WORD. I have had times of stumbling along the way, but HE has provided grace to sustain our fellowship.

HEART

Chapter 3

In order to have a concept of who GOD is, I have to know HIS motives, and what prompts HIM to act for my good. HIS WORD states the fruit of the SPIRIT is the way I attract GOD's attention, so when I yield to the fruit of the SPIRIT, HE acts to my benefit. Kindness in word and deed, soundness of mind, and redemption of my transgressions against others as well as being ready to forgive their transgressions against me.

A

Galatians 5:22-23, "But the fruit of the SPIRIT is love, joy, peace, longsuffering, kindness, goodness, faithfulness, meekness, self-control; against such there is no law."

Ω

David understood the responsibility of his own sin, and that sin **always** costs personal sustenance. Growing up I had heard people say that David was a man after GOD's own heart, but I thought that exclusively meant David was inherently born with GOD's character. Later I realized that a man after GOD's own heart also implies to give chase like pursuing someone in a game of tag except I am spiritually pursuing GOD. David was inquisitive about what motivates GOD to act, and his understanding of GOD was from both the scriptures of his day, and the personal experiences of GOD's WORD fulfilled in his life.

A

2 Samuel 24:1-25, "And again the anger of JEHOVAH was kindled against Israel, and he moved David against them, saying, Go, number Israel and Judah. And the king said to Joab the captain of the host, who was with him, Go now to and fro through all the tribes of Israel, from Dan even to Beer-sheba, and number ye the people, that I may know the sum of the people. And Joab said unto the king, Now JEHOVAH thy GOD add unto the people, how many soever they may be, a hundredfold; and may the eyes of my lord the king see it: but why doth my lord the king delight in this thing? Notwithstanding, the king's word prevailed against Joab, and against the captains of the host. And Joab and the captains of the host went out from the presence of the king, to number the people of Israel. And they passed over the Jordan, and encamped in Aroer, on the right side of the city that is in the middle of the valley of Gad, and unto Jazer: then they came to Gilead, and to the land of Tahtim-hodshi; and they came to Dan-jaan, and round about to Sidon, and came to the stronghold of Tyre, and to all the cities of the Hivites, and of the Canaanites; and they went out to the south of Judah, at Beer-sheba. So when they had gone to and fro through all the land, they came to Jerusalem at the end of nine months and twenty days. And Joab gave up the sum of the numbering of the people unto the king: and there were in Israel eight hundred thousand valiant men that drew the sword; and the men of Judah were five hundred thousand men. And David's heart smote him after that he had numbered the people. And David said unto JEHOVAH, I have sinned greatly in that which I have done: but now, O JEHOVAH, put away, I beseech thee, the iniquity of thy servant; for I have done very foolishly. And when David rose up in the morning, the word of JEHOVAH came unto the prophet Gad, David's seer, saying, Go and speak unto David, Thus saith JEHOVAH, I offer thee three things: choose thee one of them, that I may do it unto thee. So Gad came to David, and told him, and said unto him, Shall seven years of famine come unto thee in thy land? or wilt thou flee three months before thy foes while they pursue thee? or shall there be three days' pestilence in thy land? now advise thee, and consider what answer I shall return to him that sent me. And David said unto Gad, I am in a great strait: let us fall now into the hand of JEHOVAH; for his mercies are great; and let me not fall into the hand of man. So JEHOVAH sent a pestilence upon Israel from the morning even to the time appointed; and there died of the people from Dan even to

14

Beer-sheba seventy thousand men. And when the angel stretched out his hand toward Jerusalem to destroy it, JEHOVAH repented him of the evil, and said to the angel that destroyed the people, It is enough; now stay thy hand. And the angel of JEHOVAH was by the threshing-floor of Araunah the Jebusite. And David spake unto JEHOVAH when he saw the angel that smote the people, and said, Lo, I have sinned, and I have done perversely; but these sheep, what have they done? let thy hand, I pray thee, be against me, and against my father's house. And Gad came that day to David, and said unto him, Go up, rear an altar unto JEHOVAH in the threshing-floor of Araunah the Jebusite. And David went up according to the saying of Gad, as JEHOVAH commanded. And Araunah looked forth, and saw the king and his servants coming on toward him: and Araunah went out, and bowed himself before the king with his face to the ground. And Araunah said, Wherefore is my lord the king come to his servant? And David said, To buy the threshing-floor of thee, to build an altar unto JEHOVAH, that the plague may be stayed from the people. And Araunah said unto David, Let my lord the king take and offer up what seemeth good unto him: behold, the oxen for the burnt-offering, and the threshing instruments and the yokes of the oxen for the wood: all this, O king, doth Araunah give unto the king. And Araunah said unto the king, JEHOVAH thy GOD accept thee. **And the king said unto Araunah, Nay; but I will verily buy it of thee at a price. Neither will I offer burnt-offerings unto JEHOVAH my GOD which cost me nothing.** So David bought the threshing-floor and the oxen for fifty shekels of silver. And David built there an altar unto JEHOVAH, and offered burnt-offerings and peace-offerings. So JEHOVAH was entreated for the land, and the plague was stayed from Israel."

$$\Omega$$

GOD values life because he is living, and desires me to be living as well. Second, GOD's humility provides an avenue of peace regardless of my disposition. Third GOD, loves righteousness, and rewards or chastises me according to my obedience. Fourth, GOD's patience forges consistent character allowing me to yield to HIS sovereignty.

Fifth, GOD is faithful to HIS WORD even if I do not like certain outcomes, and HE is ready to restore me if I mess up. Sixth, GOD longs to have a relationship with me. Lastly, GOD's wisdom creates and balances all things to reconcile justice. GOD's values are to be viewed like facets in a diamond. I am not to see a value as one that takes precedence over the other, rather pure qualities from different aspects.

LIFE

Chapter 4

GOD is living, and even before creation HE has always been living. HE is absolutely self-aware that HE is living, and from creation HE has empowered life. It was not until after Adam ate from the tree of knowledge that death progressed from being abstract thought into concrete reality. Before death entered into history, GOD already had a plan to eliminate it by HIS own sacrifice on the cross.

That is how valuable life is to GOD. None of HIS promises come to fruition without the life of Isaac from Abraham and Sarah including the lives after Isaac. Is life important to GOD even though people are flawed? Yes. Now, is my life important to GOD? Yes. This is a journey through the creation of life. On the third day GOD created plant life, on the fifth day fowls and sea life, and on the sixth day insects, animals, and man.

A

Genesis 1:11-13, "And GOD said, Let the earth put forth grass, herbs yielding seed, and fruit-trees bearing fruit after their kind, wherein is the seed thereof, upon the earth: and it was so. And the earth brought forth grass, herbs yielding seed after their kind, and trees bearing fruit, wherein is the seed thereof, after their kind: and GOD saw that it was good. And there was evening and there was morning, a third day."

Genesis 1:20-31, "And GOD said, Let the waters swarm with swarms of living creatures, and let birds fly above the earth in the open firmament of heaven. And GOD created the great sea-monsters, and every living creature that moveth, wherewith the waters swarmed, after their kind, and every winged bird after its kind: and GOD saw that it was good. And GOD blessed them, saying, Be fruitful, and multiply, and fill the waters in the seas, and let birds multiply on the earth. And there was evening and there was morning, a fifth day. And GOD said, Let the earth bring forth living creatures after their kind, cattle, and creeping things, and beasts of the earth after their kind: and it was so. And GOD made the beasts of the earth after their kind, and the cattle after their kind, and everything that creepeth upon the ground after its kind: and GOD saw that it was good. And GOD said, Let US make man in OUR image, after OUR likeness: and let them have dominion over the fish of the sea, and over the birds of the heavens, and over the cattle, and over all the earth, and over every creeping thing that creepeth upon the earth. And GOD created man in HIS own image, in the image of GOD created HE him; male and female created HE them. And GOD blessed them: and GOD said unto them, Be fruitful, and multiply, and replenish the earth, and subdue it; and have dominion over the fish of the sea, and over the birds of the heavens, and over every living thing that moveth upon the earth. And GOD said, Behold, I have given you every herb yielding seed, which is upon the face of all the earth, and every tree, in which is the fruit of a tree yielding seed; to you it shall be for food: and to every beast of the earth, and to every bird of the heavens, and to everything that creepeth upon the earth, wherein there is life, I have given every green herb for food: and it was so. And GOD saw everything that HE had made, and, behold, it was very good. And there was evening and there was morning, the sixth day."

Ω

GOD is the creator and pursuer of life, and therefore the implication is that HE enjoys the life that HE has given to HIS creation. HE states that all HE created is very good including me, and that indicates that HE inherently delights in me. HIS first impression of me is that I am very good, and as I conform to HIS image the more I please HIM. JESUS confirms this idea of pleasing GOD by loving those who love HIM.

A

John 8:28-42, "JESUS therefore said, When ye have lifted up the SON of man, then shall ye know that I am HE, and that I do nothing of MYSELF, but as the FATHER taught me, I speak these things. And HE that sent ME is with ME; HE hath not left ME alone; for I do always the things that are pleasing to HIM. As HE spake these things, many believed on HIM. JESUS therefore said to those Jews that had believed HIM, If ye abide in MY word, then are ye truly MY disciples; and ye shall know the truth, and the truth shall make you free. They answered unto HIM, We are Abraham's seed, and have never yet been in bondage to any man: how sayest THOU, Ye shall be made free? JESUS answered them, Verily, verily, I say unto you, Every one that committeth sin is the bondservant of sin. And the bondservant abideth not in the house for ever: the SON abideth for ever. If therefore the SON shall make you free, ye shall be free indeed. I know that ye are Abraham's seed: yet ye seek to kill ME, because MY WORD hath not free course in you. I speak the things which I have seen with MY FATHER: and ye also do the things which ye heard from your father. They answered and said unto HIM, Our father is Abraham. JESUS saith unto them, If ye were Abraham's children, ye would do the works of Abraham. But now ye seek to kill ME, a man that hath told you the truth, which I heard from GOD: this did not Abraham. Ye do the works of your father. They said unto HIM, We were not born of fornication; we have one FATHER, even GOD. JESUS said unto them, If GOD were your FATHER, ye would love ME: for I came forth and am come from GOD; for neither have I come of MYSELF, but HE sent ME."

Ω

GOD is generous to all who value life. HE creates life, and desires me to value HIS work. The CREATOR of life honors those (Jewish and gentile) who preserve life, even if questionable methods are used to do so.

A

19

Exodus 1:15-21, "And the king of Egypt spake to the Hebrew mid-wives, of whom the name of the one was Shiphrah, and the name of the other Puah: and he said, When ye do the office of a midwife to the Hebrew women, and see them upon the birth-stool; if it be a son, then ye shall kill him; but if it be a daughter, then she shall live. But the midwives feared GOD, and did not as the king of Egypt com-manded them, but saved the men-children alive. And the king of Egypt called for the midwives, and said unto them, Why have ye done this thing, and have saved the men-children alive? And the midwives said unto Pharaoh, Because the Hebrew women are not as the Egyp-tian women; for they are lively, and are delivered ere the midwife come unto them. And GOD dealt well with the midwives: and the people multiplied, and waxed very mighty. And it came to pass, be-cause the midwives feared GOD, that HE made them households."

Ω

The manifestation of GOD's power is life. Life is the hallmark of GOD's presence. GOD accentuates HIS affinity towards life by using HIS power to keep both Enoch and Elijah from ever experienc-ing death.

A

Genesis 5:21-24, "And Enoch lived sixty and five years, and begat Methuselah: and Enoch walked with GOD after he begat Methuselah three hundred years, and begat sons and daughters: and all the days of Enoch were three hundred sixty and five years: and Enoch walked with GOD: and he was not; for GOD took him."

2 Kings 2:8-11, "And Elijah took his mantle, and wrapped it together, and smote the waters, and they were divided hither and thither, so that they two went over on dry ground. And it came to pass, when they were gone over, that Elijah said unto Elisha, Ask what I shall do for thee, before I am taken from thee. And Elisha said, I pray thee, let a double portion of thy spirit be upon me. And he said, Thou hast asked a hard thing: nevertheless, if thou see me when I am taken from thee, it shall be so unto thee; but if not, it shall not be so. And it came to pass, as they still went on, and talked, that, behold, there appeared a chariot of fire, and horses of fire, which parted them both asunder; and Elijah went up by a whirlwind into heaven."

Ω

Moses implored the children of Israel to choose life, which acknowledged Enoch's **choice** of life. His conclusion from Enoch's life was that death was optional. Moses knew that GOD empowers life with boundless possibly.

A

Deuteronomy 30:19-20, "I call heaven and earth to witness against you this day, that I have set before thee life and death, the blessing and the curse: therefore choose life, that thou mayest live, thou and thy seed; to love JEHOVAH thy GOD, to obey HIS voice, and to cleave unto HIM; for HE is thy life, and the length of thy days; that thou mayest dwell in the land which JEHOVAH sware unto thy fathers, to Abraham, to Isaac, and to Jacob, to give them."

Ω

Before entering "The Promise Land" Moses instructed Israel to destroy the inhabitants, and not to allow their sons and daughters marry the people of the land. That is what Moses stated; however, is that what the LORD commanded, or is that what Moses interpreted? The LORD says overthrow their idols, which sounds more like invalidating their governments and cultures of worship after all the LORD said HE would destroy and drive out the inhabitants of the land.

A

Exodus 23:24, (GOD speaking) "Thou shalt not bow down to their gods, nor serve them, nor do after their works; but thou shalt utterly overthrow them, and break in pieces their pillars."

Exodus 23:27-30, (GOD speaking) "I will send MY terror before thee, and will discomfit all the people to whom thou shalt come, and I will make all thine enemies turn their backs unto thee. And I will send the hornet before thee, which shall drive out the Hivite, the Canaanite, and the Hittite, from before thee. I will not drive them out from before thee in one year, lest the land become desolate, and the beasts of the field multiply against thee. By little and little I will drive them out from before thee, until thou be increased, and inherit the land."

Deuteronomy 7:1-4, (Moses speaking) "When JEHOVAH thy GOD shall bring thee into the land whither thou goest to possess it, and shall cast out many nations before thee, the Hittite, and the Girgashite, and the Amorite, and the Canaanite, and the Perizzite, and the Hivite, and the Jebusite, seven nations greater and mightier than thou; and when JEHOVAH thy GOD shall deliver them up before thee, and thou shalt smite them; then thou shalt utterly destroy them: thou shalt make no covenant with them, nor show mercy unto them; neither shalt thou make marriages with them; thy daughter thou shalt not give unto his son, nor his daughter shalt thou take unto thy son. For he will turn away thy son from following me, that they may serve other gods: so will the anger of JEHOVAH be kindled against you, and HE will destroy thee quickly."

Deuteronomy 20:10-18, (Moses speaking) "When thou drawest nigh unto a city to fight against it, then proclaim peace unto it. And it shall be, if it make thee answer of peace, and open unto thee, then it shall be, that all the people that are found therein shall become tributary unto thee, and shall serve thee. And if it will make no peace with thee, but will make war against thee, then thou shalt besiege it: and when JEHOVAH thy GOD delivereth it into thy hand, thou shalt smite every male thereof with the edge of the sword: but the women, and the little ones, and the cattle, and all that is in the city, even all the spoil thereof, shalt thou take for a prey unto thyself; and thou shalt eat the spoil of thine enemies, which JEHOVAH thy GOD hath given thee. Thus shalt thou do unto all the cities which are very far off from thee, which are not of the cities of these nations. But of the cities of these peoples, that JEHOVAH thy GOD giveth thee for an inheritance, thou shalt save alive nothing that breatheth; but thou shalt utterly destroy them: the Hittite, and the Amorite, the Canaanite, and the Perizzite, the Hivite, and the Jebusite; as JEHOVAH thy GOD hath commanded thee; that they teach you not to do after all their abominations, which they have done unto their gods; so would ye sin against JEHOVAH your GOD. When thou shalt besiege a city a long time, in making war against it to take it, thou shalt not destroy the trees thereof by wielding an axe against them; for thou mayest eat of them, and thou shalt not cut them down; for is the tree of the field man, that it should be besieged of thee? Only the trees of which thou knowest that they are not trees for food, thou shalt destroy and cut them down; and thou shalt build bulwarks against the city that maketh war with thee, until it fall."

Ω

To further validate the point that GOD did not want to destroy everyone, upon first entering "The Promise Land" Rahab's entire family is allowed to live. I ask myself, if GOD wanted the children of Israel to destroy all the people of Canaan, then why before the first battle is HIS first act to preserve life.

The LORD validates saving Rahab's life, a supposed to be dead gentile, by including her in the lineage of King David, who is also in the lineage of JESUS. After her comes Ruth, a cursed Moabite, who marries Boaz, a blessed Hebrew. Ruth is also in both the lineage of King David and JESUS, so in conclusion GOD has an affinity towards life. Remember Moses states not to marry people outside their culture.

Joshua 2:1-20, "And Joshua the son of Nun sent out of Shittim two men as spies secretly, saying, Go, view the land, and Jericho. And they went and came into the house of a harlot whose name was Rahab, and lay there. And it was told the king of Jericho, saying, Behold, there came men in hither to-night of the children of Israel to search out the land. And the king of Jericho sent unto Rahab, saying, Bring forth the men that are come to thee, that are entered into thy house; for they are come to search out all the land. And the woman took the two men, and hid them; and she said, Yea, the men came unto me, but I knew not whence they were: and it came to pass about the time of the shutting of the gate, when it was dark, that the men went out; whither the men went I know not: pursue after them quickly; for ye will overtake them. But she had brought them up to the roof, and hid them with the stalks of flax, which she had laid in order upon the roof. And the men pursued after them the way to the Jordan unto the fords: and as soon as they that pursued after them were gone out, they shut the gate. And before they were laid down, she came up unto them upon the roof; and she said unto the men, I know that JEHOVAH hath given you the land, and that the fear of you is fallen upon us, and that all the inhabitants of the land melt away before you. For we have heard how JEHOVAH dried up the water of the Red Sea before you, when ye came out of Egypt; and what ye did unto the two kings of the Amorites, that were beyond the Jordan, unto Sihon and to Og, whom ye utterly destroyed. And as soon as we had heard it, our hearts did melt, neither did there remain any more spirit in any man, because of you: for JEHOVAH your GOD, HE is GOD in heaven above, and on earth beneath. Now therefore, I pray you, swear unto me by JEHOVAH, since I have dealt kindly with you, that ye also will deal kindly with my father's house, and give me a true token; and that ye will save alive my father, and my mother, and my brethren, and my sisters, and all that they have, and will deliver our lives from death. And the men said unto her, Our life for yours, if ye utter not this our business; and it shall be, when JEHOVAH giveth us the land, that we will deal kindly and truly with thee. Then she let them down by a cord through the window: for her house was upon the side of the wall, and she dwelt upon the wall. And she said unto them, Get you to the mountain, lest the pursuers light upon you; and hide yourselves there three days, until the pursuers be returned: and afterward may ye go your way. And the men said unto her, We will be guiltless of this thine oath which thou hast made us to swear. Behold, when we come into the land, thou shalt bind this line of scarlet thread in the window which thou didst let us down by: and thou shalt gather unto thee into the house thy father, and thy mother, and thy brethren, and all thy father's household. And it shall be, that whosoever shall go out of the doors of thy house into the street, his blood shall be upon his head, and we shall be guiltless: and whosoever shall be with thee in the house, his blood shall be on our head, if any hand be upon him. But if thou utter this our business, then we shall be guiltless of thine oath which thou hast made us to swear."

Matthew 1:1-16, "The book of the generation of JESUS CHRIST, the son of David, the son of Abraham. Abraham begat Isaac; and Isaac begat Jacob; and Jacob begat Judah and his brethren; and Judah begat Perez and Zerah of Tamar; and Perez begat Hezron; and Hezron begat Ram; and Ram begat Amminadab; and Amminadab begat Nahshon; and Nahshon begat Salmon; **and Salmon begat Boaz of Rahab; and Boaz begat Obed of Ruth;** and Obed begat Jesse; and Jesse begat David the king. and Solomon begat Rehoboam; and Rehoboam begat Abijah; and Abijah begat Asa; and Asa begat Jehoshaphat; and Jehoshaphat begat Joram; and Joram begat Uzziah; and Uzziah begat Jotham; and Jotham begat Ahaz; and Ahaz begat Hezekiah; and Hezekiah begat Manasseh; and Manasseh begat Amon; and Amon begat Josiah; and Josiah begat Jechoniah and his brethren, at the time of the carrying away to Babylon. And after the carrying away to Babylon, Jechoniah begat Shealtiel; and Shealtiel begat Zerubbabel; and Zerubbabel begat Abiud; and Abiud begat Eliakim; and Eliakim begat Azor; and Azor begat Sadoc; and Sadoc begat Achim; and Achim begat Eliud; and Eliud begat Eleazar; and Eleazar begat Matthan; and

Matthan begat Jacob; and Jacob begat Joseph the husband of Mary, of whom was born JESUS, who is called CHRIST."

Ω

The people of Gibeon were allowed to live even though they deceived the children of Israel. They tricked Joshua to keep themselves alive, but they forfeited their government and culture. Again, was this Moses interpretation to destroy everyone, or did GOD have another intention? They willingly accepted lives of servitude.

A

Joshua 9:3-27, "But when the inhabitants of Gibeon heard what Joshua had done unto Jericho and to Ai, they also did work wilily, and went and made as if they had been ambassadors, and took old sacks upon their asses, and wine-skins, old and rent and bound up, and old and patched shoes upon their feet, and old garments upon them; and all the bread of their provision was dry and was become mouldy. And they went to Joshua unto the camp at Gilgal, and said unto him, and to the men of Israel, We are come from a far country: now therefore make ye a covenant with us. And the men of Israel said unto the Hivites, Peradventure ye dwell among us; and how shall we make a covenant with you? And they said unto Joshua, We are thy servants. And Joshua said unto them, Who are ye? and from whence come ye? And they said unto him, From a very far country thy servants are come because of the name of JEHOVAH thy GOD: for we have heard the fame of HIM, and all that HE did in Egypt, and all that HE did to the two kings of the Amorites, that were beyond the Jordan, to Sihon king of Heshbon, and to Og king of Bashan, who was at Ashtaroth. And our elders and all the inhabitants of our country spake to us, saying, Take provision in your hand for the journey, and go to meet them, and say unto them, We are your servants: and now make ye a covenant with us. This our bread we took hot for our provision out of our houses on the day we came forth to go unto you; but now,

26

behold, it is dry, and is become mouldy: and these wine-skins, which we filled, were new; and, behold, they are rent: and these our garments and our shoes are become old by reason of the very long journey. And the men took of their provision, and asked not counsel at the mouth of JEHOVAH. And Joshua made peace with them, and made a covenant with them, to let them live: and the princes of the congregation sware unto them. And it came to pass at the end of three days after they had made a covenant with them, that they heard that they were their neighbors, and that they dwelt among them. And the children of Israel journeyed, and came unto their cities on the third day. Now their cities were Gibeon, and Chephirah, and Beeroth, and Kiriath-jearim. And the children of Israel smote them not, because the princes of the congregation had sworn unto them by JEHOVAH, the GOD of Israel. And all the congregation murmured against the princes. But all the princes said unto all the congregation, We have sworn unto them by JEHOVAH, the GOD of Israel: now therefore we may not touch them. This we will do to them, and let them live; lest wrath be upon us, because of the oath which we sware unto them. And the princes said unto them, Let them live: so they became hewers of wood and drawers of water unto all the congregation, as the princes had spoken unto them. And Joshua called for them, and he spake unto them, saying, Wherefore have ye beguiled us, saying, We are very far from you; when ye dwell among us? Now therefore ye are cursed, and there shall never fail to be of you bondmen, both hewers of wood and drawers of water for the house of my GOD. And they answered Joshua, and said, Because it was certainly told thy servants, how that JEHOVAH thy GOD commanded HIS servant Moses to give you all the land, and to destroy all the inhabitants of the land from before you; therefore we were sore afraid for our lives because of you, and have done this thing. And now, behold, we are in thy hand: as it seemeth good and right unto thee to do unto us, do. And so did he unto them, and delivered them out of the hand of the children of Israel, that they slew them not. And Joshua made them that day hewers of wood and drawers of water for the congregation, and for the altar of JEHOVAH, unto this day, in the place which HE should choose."

Ω

For centuries people identify their god by a manifestation of death. Because in war, gods were called upon to destroy rivals. When educated in that manner, people devolve to a survivalist model with individualized strata of hierarchy. JESUS had to scold his disciples for falling prey to that idea.

A

Luke 9:51-55, "And it came to pass, when the days were well-nigh come that HE (JESUS) should be received up, HE stedfastly set HIS face to go to Jerusalem, and sent messengers before HIS face: and they went, and entered into a village of the Samaritans, to make ready for HIM. And they did not receive HIM, because HIS face was as though HE were going to Jerusalem. And when HIS disciples James and John saw this, they said, LORD, wilt THOU that we bid fire to come down from heaven, and consume them? But HE turned, and rebuked them."

Ω

GOD is not satisfied with sacrifices of death. HIS desire is the sacrifice of life. My biological dad died by ending his life with the idea that my mother, sister, and I lives were going to be better without him, but the man I call "Dad" lived for us by improving our lives with his own life. What good would JESUS' death on the cross be if he had not lived an unblemished life? Yes, JESUS died, but my perspective is HIS sacrifice was HIS life, not to simply die.

A

John 10:7-10, "JESUS therefore said unto them again, Verily, verily, I say unto you, I am the door of the sheep. All that came before me are thieves and robbers: but the sheep did not hear them. I am the

28

DOOR; by ME if any man enter in, he shall be saved, and shall go in and go out, and shall find pasture. The thief cometh not, but that he may steal, and kill, and destroy: I came that they may have life, and may have it abundantly."

John 15:11-13, (JESUS speaking) "These things have I spoken unto you, that MY joy may be in you, and that your joy may be made full. This is MY commandment, that ye love one another, even as I have loved you. Greater love hath no man than this, that a man lay down his life for his friends."

Ω

JESUS is neither satisfied with me simply being alive, nor having a lot in life, but HE wants my life to overflow. HE has so much life it pours out of HIM. HIS life is uncontainable, and HIS desire is for me to share it.

HUMILITY

Chapter 5

Humility is how GOD manifests HIMSELF to me. He is KING of kings, LORD of lords, ALPHA and OMEGA, the BEGINNING and the ENDING, the ALMIGHTY, and HIS desire is for me to believe HE wants me to flourish. GOD humbles HIMSELF to be proactive with HIS creation instead of being aloof and out of touch. JESUS touches my infirmities, and after HIS resurrection HE retains HIS wounds as a remembrance of my disposition. I am flawed, but HE is empowering me to overcome myself. Abraham humbled himself to GOD, and left his father's house.

A

Genesis 12:1-4, "Now JEHOVAH said unto Abram, Get thee out of thy country, and from thy kindred, and from thy father's house, unto the land that I will show thee: and I will make of thee a great nation, and I will bless thee, and make thy name great; and be thou a blessing; and I will bless them that bless thee, and him that curseth thee will I curse: and in thee shall all the families of the earth be blessed. So Abram went, as JEHOVAH had spoken unto him; and Lot went with him: and Abram was seventy and five years old when he departed out of Haran."

Ω

Isaac humbled himself giving up wells that he had dug, for a peaceful coexistence with his neighbors. Jacob knew he had to return to the place GOD promises to Abraham, so he humbled himself to his brother, Esau, to live in peace by calling himself servant and Esau lord. Judah humbled himself to deliver Benjamin, his brother, from imprisonment. Even after Joseph's brothers treated him poorly, he humbled himself to keep his father's household alive.

A

Genesis 26:17-22, "And Isaac departed thence, and encamped in the valley of Gerar, and dwelt there. And Isaac digged again the wells of water, which they had digged in the days of Abraham his father. For the Philistines had stopped them after the death of Abraham. And he called their names after the names by which his father had called them. And Isaac's servants digged in the valley, and found there a well of springing water. And the herdsmen of Gerar strove with Isaac's herdsmen, saying, The water is ours. And he called the name of the well Esek, because they contended with him. And they digged another well, and they strove for that also. And he called the name of it Sitnah. And he removed from thence, and digged another well. And for that they strove not. And he called the name of it Rehoboth. And he said, For now JEHOVAH hath made room for us, and we shall be fruitful in the land."

Genesis 32:9-33:16, "And Jacob said, O GOD of my father Abraham, and GOD of my father Isaac, O JEHOVAH, who saidst unto me, Return unto thy country, and to thy kindred, and I will do thee good: I am not worthy of the least of all the lovingkindnesses, and of all the truth, which THOU hast showed unto thy servant; for with my staff I passed over this Jordan; and now I am become two companies. Deliver me, I pray THEE, from the hand of my brother, from the hand of Esau: for I fear him, lest he come and smite me, the mother with the children. And THOU saidst, I will surely do thee good, and make thy SEED as the sand of the sea, which cannot be numbered for multitude. And he lodged there that night, and took of that which he had with him a present for Esau his brother: two hundred she-goats and twenty he-goats, two hundred ewes and twenty rams, thirty milch camels and their colts, forty cows and ten bulls, twenty she-asses and ten foals. And he delivered them into the hand of his servants, every drove by itself, and said unto his servants, Pass over before me, and put a space betwixt drove and drove. And he commanded the foremost, saying, When Esau my brother meeteth thee, and asketh thee, saying, Whose art thou? and whither goest thou? and whose are these before thee? then thou shalt say, They are **thy servant** Jacob's; it is a present sent unto **my lord** Esau: and, behold, he also is behind us. And he commanded also the second, and the third, and all that followed the droves, saying, On this manner shall ye speak unto Esau, when ye find him; and ye shall say, Moreover, behold, **thy servant** Jacob is behind us. For he said, I will appease him with the present that goeth before me, and afterward I will see his face; peradventure he will accept me. So the present passed over before him: and he himself lodged that night in the company. And he rose up that night, and took his two wives, and his two handmaids, and his eleven children, and passed over the ford of the Jabbok. And he took them, and sent them over the stream, and sent over that which he had. And Jacob was left alone; and there wrestled a MAN with him until the breaking of the day. And when he saw that he prevailed not against HIM, HE touched the hollow of his thigh; and the hollow of Jacob's thigh was strained, as HE wrestled with him. And HE said, Let ME go, for the day breaketh. And he said, I will not let THEE go, except THOU bless me. And HE said unto him, What is thy name? And he said, Jacob. And HE said, Thy name shall be called no more Jacob, but Israel: for thou hast striven with GOD and with men, and hast prevailed. And Jacob asked HIM, and said, Tell me, I pray THEE, THY name. And HE said, Wherefore is it that thou dost ask after MY name? And HE blessed him there. And Jacob called the name of the place Peniel: for, said he, I have seen GOD face to face, and my life is preserved. And the sun rose upon him as he passed over Penuel, and he limped upon his thigh. Therefore the children of Israel eat not the sinew of the hip which is upon the hollow of the thigh, unto this day: because HE touched the hollow of Jacob's thigh in the sinew of the hip. And Jacob lifted up his eyes, and looked, and, behold, Esau was coming, and with him four hundred men. And he divided the children unto Leah, and unto Rachel, and unto the two handmaids. And he put the handmaids and their children foremost, and Leah and her children after, and Rachel and Joseph hindermost. And he himself passed over before them, and bowed himself to the ground seven times, until he came near to his brother. And Esau ran to meet him, and embraced him, and fell on his neck, and kissed him: and they wept. And he lifted up his eyes, and saw the women and the children; and said, Who are these with thee? And he said, The children whom GOD hath graciously given **thy servant**. Then the handmaids came near, they and their children, and they bowed themselves. And Leah also and her children came near, and bowed themselves: and after came Joseph near and Rachel, and they bowed themselves. And he said, What meanest thou by all this company which I met? And he said, To find favor in the sight of **my lord**. And Esau said, I have enough, my brother; let that which thou hast be thine. And Jacob said, Nay, I pray thee, if now I have found favor in thy sight, then receive my present at my hand; forasmuch as I have seen thy face, as one seeth the face of GOD, and thou wast pleased with me. Take, I pray thee, my gift that is brought to thee; because GOD hath dealt graciously with me, and because I have enough. And he urged him, and he took it. And he said, Let us take our journey, and let us go, and I will go before thee. And he said unto him, **My lord** knoweth that the children are tender, and that the flocks and herds with me have their young: and if they overdrive them one day, all the flocks will die. Let **my lord**, I pray thee, pass over before **his servant**: and I will lead on gently, according to the pace of the cattle that are before me and according to the pace of the children, until I come unto **my lord** unto Seir. And Esau said, Let me now leave with thee some of the folk that are with me. And he said, What needeth it? let me find favor in the sight of **my lord**. So Esau returned that day on his way unto Seir."

Genesis 37:23-28, "And it came to pass, when Joseph was come unto his brethren, that they stripped Joseph of his coat, the coat of many colors that was on him; and they took him, and cast him into the pit: and the pit was empty, there was no water in it. And they sat down to eat bread: and they lifted up their eyes and looked, and, behold, a caravan of Ishmaelites was coming from Gilead, with their camels bearing spicery and balm and myrrh, going to carry it down to Egypt. And Judah said unto his brethren, What profit is it if we slay our brother and conceal his blood? Come, and let us sell him to the Ishmaelites, and let not our hand be upon him; for he is our brother, our flesh. And his brethren hearkened unto him. And there passed by Midianites, merchantmen; and they drew and lifted up Joseph out of the pit, and sold Joseph to the Ishmaelites for twenty pieces of silver. And they brought Joseph into Egypt."

Genesis 43:6-10, "And Israel said, Wherefore dealt ye so ill with me, as to tell the man whether ye had yet a brother? And they said, The man asked straitly concerning ourselves, and concerning our kindred, saying, Is your father yet alive? have ye another brother? And we told him according to the tenor of these words: could we in any wise know that he would say, Bring your brother down? And Judah said unto Israel his father, Send the lad with me, and we will arise and go; that we may live, and not die, both we, and thou, and also our little ones. I will be surety for him; of my hand shalt thou require him: if I bring him not unto thee, and set him before thee, then let me bear the blame for ever: for except we had lingered, surely we had now returned a second time."

Genesis 44:16-34, "And Judah said, What shall we say unto my lord? what shall we speak? or how shall we clear ourselves? GOD hath found out the iniquity of thy servants: behold, we are my lord's bond-men, both we, and he also in whose hand the cup is found. And he said, Far be it from me that I should do so: the man in whose hand the cup is found, he shall be my bondman; but as for you, get you up in peace unto your father. Then Judah came near unto him, and said, Oh, my lord, let thy servant, I pray thee, speak a word in my lord's ears, and let not thine anger burn against thy servant; for thou art even as Pharaoh. My lord asked his servants, saying, Have ye a father, or a brother? And we said unto my lord, We have a father, an old man, and a child of his old age, a little one; and his brother is dead, and he alone is left of his mother; and his father loveth him. And thou saidst unto thy servants, Bring him down unto me, that I may set mine eyes upon him. And we said unto my lord, The lad cannot leave his father: for if he should leave his father, his father would die. And thou saidst unto thy servants, Except your youngest brother come down with you, ye shall see my face no more. And it came to pass when we came

34

up unto thy servant my father, we told him the words of my lord. And our father said, Go again, buy us a little food. And we said, We cannot go down: if our youngest brother be with us, then will we go down: for we may not see the man's face, expect our youngest brother be with us. And thy servant my father said unto us, Ye know that my wife bare me two sons: and the one went out from me, and I said, Surely he is torn in pieces; and I have not seen him since: and if ye take this one also from me, and harm befall him, ye will bring down my gray hairs with sorrow to Sheol. Now therefore when I come to thy servant my father, and the lad is not with us; seeing that his life is bound up in the lad's life; it will come to pass, when he seeth that the lad is not with us, that he will die: and thy servants will bring down the gray hairs of thy servant our father with sorrow to Sheol. For thy servant became surety for the lad unto my father, saying, If I bring him not unto thee, then shall I bear the blame to my father for ever. Now therefore, let thy servant, I pray thee, abide instead of the lad a bondman to my lord; and let the lad go up with his brethren. For how shall I go up to my father, if the lad be not with me? lest I see the evil that shall come on my father."

Genesis 45:1-11, "Then Joseph could not refrain himself before all them that stood before him; and he cried, Cause every man to go out from me. And there stood no man with him, while Joseph made himself known unto his brethren. And he wept aloud: and the Egyptians heard, and the house of Pharaoh heard. And Joseph said unto his brethren, I am Joseph; doth my father yet live? And his brethren could not answer him; for they were troubled at his presence. And Joseph said unto his brethren, Come near to me, I pray you. And they came near. And he said, I am Joseph your brother, whom ye sold into Egypt. And now be not grieved, nor angry with yourselves, that ye sold me hither: for GOD did send me before you to preserve life. For these two years hath the famine been in the land: and there are yet five years, in which there shall be neither plowing nor harvest. And GOD sent me before you to preserve you a remnant in the earth, and to save you alive by a great deliverance. So now it was not you that sent me hither, but GOD: and he hath made me a father to Pharaoh, and lord of all his house, and ruler over all the land of Egypt. Haste ye, and go up to my father, and say unto him, Thus saith thy son Joseph, GOD hath made me lord of all Egypt: come down unto me, tarry not; and thou shalt dwell in the land of Goshen, and thou shalt be near unto me, thou, and thy children, and thy children's children, and thy flocks, and thy herds, and all that thou hast: and there will I nourish thee; for there are yet five years of famine; lest thou come to poverty, thou, and thy household, and all that thou hast."

Ω

Moses humbled himself to go back to Egypt, and ask Pharaoh to release HIS people. Saul did not humble himself to be obedient. Samuel tells Saul the LORD has sought a man after GOD's own heart in reference to David. David understood that humility motivates GOD to intervene.

A

Exodus 4:18-23, "And Moses went and returned to Jethro his father-in-law, and said unto him, Let me go, I pray thee, and return unto my brethren that are in Egypt, and see whether they be yet alive. And Jethro said to Moses, Go in peace. And JEHOVAH said unto Moses in Midian, Go, return into Egypt; for all the men are dead that sought thy life. And Moses took his wife and his sons, and set them upon an ass, and he returned to the land of Egypt: and Moses took the rod of GOD in his hand. And JEHOVAH said unto Moses, When thou goest back into Egypt, see that thou do before Pharaoh all the wonders which I have put in thy hand: but I will harden his heart and he will not let the people go. And thou shalt say unto Pharaoh, Thus saith JEHOVAH, Israel is MY son, MY first-born: and I have said unto thee, Let MY son go, that he may serve ME; and thou hast refused to let him go: behold, I will slay thy son, thy first-born."

1 Samuel 13:13-14, "And Samuel said to Saul, Thou hast done foolishly; thou hast not kept the commandment of JEHOVAH thy GOD, which HE commanded thee: for now would JEHOVAH have established thy kingdom upon Israel for ever. But now thy kingdom shall not continue: JEHOVAH hath sought HIM a man after HIS own heart, and JEHOVAH hath appointed HIM to be prince over HIS people, because thou hast not kept that which JEHOVAH commanded thee."

2 Samuel 16:5-13, "And when king David came to Bahurim, behold, there came out thence a man of the family of the house of Saul, whose name was Shimei, the son of Gera; he came out, and cursed still as he came. And he cast stones at David, and at all the servants of king David: and all the people and all the mighty men were on his right hand and on his left. And thus said Shimei when he cursed, Begone, begone, thou man of blood, and base fellow: JEHOVAH hath returned upon thee all the blood of the house of Saul, in whose stead thou hast reigned; and JEHOVAH hath delivered the kingdom into the hand of Absalom thy son; and, behold, thou art taken in thine own mischief, because thou art a man of blood. Then said Abishai the son of Zeruiah unto the king, Why should this dead dog curse my lord the king? let me go over, I pray thee, and take off his head. And the king said, What have I to do with you, ye sons of Zeruiah? Because he curseth, and because JEHOVAH hath said unto him, Curse David; who then shall say, Wherefore hast thou done so? And David said to Abishai, and to all his servants, Behold, my son, who came forth from my bowels, seeketh my life: how much more may this Benjamite now do it? let him alone, and let him curse; for JEHOVAH hath bidden him. **It may be that JEHOVAH will look on the wrong done unto me, and that JEHOVAH will requite me good for his cursing of me this day.** So David and his men went by the way; and Shimei went along on the hill-side over against him, and cursed as he went, and threw stones at him, and cast dust."

Ω

As a believer of GOD's WORD, I have to convey the principles of these bible stories into my living. My mind constantly engages scripture throughout the day in order to evaluate my own actions and motives. David understood practical application of scripture.

A

Proverbs 24:17-18, "Rejoice not when thine enemy falleth, And let not thy heart be glad when he is overthrown; Lest JEHOVAH see it, and it displease HIM, And he turn away HIS wrath from him."

Isaiah 66:1-2, "Thus saith JEHOVAH, Heaven is MY throne, and the earth is MY footstool: what manner of house will ye build unto ME? and what place shall be MY rest? For all these things hath MY hand made, and so all these things came to be, saith JEHOVAH: but to this man will I look, even to HIM that is poor and of a contrite spirit, and that trembleth at MY WORD."

Ω

JESUS humbles HIMSELF by laying aside glory for humiliation, exhaustion, hunger, thirst, betrayal, and life for me. The entirety of the gospel is GOD's humility through JESUS CHRIST, so that we might have an eternity of peace. Peace does not exist without humility, so both have a direct relationship.

I cannot attain peace with my neighbor unless we are willing to humble ourselves to compromise. Both asking for forgiveness and forgiving are humble compromises. When I ask for forgiveness, I am admitting an error. When I forgive, I am relinquishing the power of retribution.

A

Philippians 2:5-8, "Have this mind in you, which was also in CHRIST JESUS: who, existing in the form of GOD, counted not the being on an equality with GOD a thing to be grasped, but emptied HIMSELF, taking the form of a servant, being made in the likeness of men; and being found in fashion as a man, HE humbled HIMSELF, becoming obedient even unto death, yea, the death of the cross."

Luke 18:9-14, "And HE (JESUS) spake also this parable unto certain who trusted in themselves that they were righteous, and set all others at nought: Two men went up into the temple to pray; the one a Pharisee, and the other a publican. The Pharisee stood and prayed thus with himself, GOD, I thank THEE, that I am not as the rest of men, extortioners, unjust, adulterers, or even as this publican. I fast twice in the week; I give tithes of all that I get. But the publican, standing afar off, would not lift up so much as his eyes unto heaven, but smote his breast, saying, GOD, be THOU merciful to me a sinner. I say unto you, This man went down to his house justified rather than the other: for every one that exalteth himself shall be humbled; but he that humbleth himself shall be exalted."

Ω

Of course, the publican humbles himself, but stop to think, does GOD have to humble HIMSELF to honor the publican's prayer? The one absolving transgressions must be humble enough to take on the risk of the liability of the transgressor. The transgressor is obligated to pay debts, but it is ignorant to believe that unresolved debt does not affect the one to whom the debt is owed. Even all-powerful GOD, compromised with me while I was a sinner in order to offer me eternal life by giving me HIS HOLY SPIRIT.

A

Romans 5:6-8, "For while we were yet weak, in due season CHRIST died for the ungodly. For scarcely for a righteous man will one die: for peradventure for the good man some one would even dare to die.

But GOD commendeth HIS own love toward us, in that, while we were yet sinners, CHRIST died for us."

Ω

GOD still willingly, humbly answers my prayers, and sure I understand that being humble puts me in a place of potential suffering, but HE has given me the COMFORTER to endure life's trials and tribulations. The HOLY SPIRIT helps me overcome afflictions. JESUS prayed to the FATHER for me to receive the HOLY SPIRIT, and that is reassuring, knowing I am able to pray for HIS absolute will.

A

John 14:13-27, "And whatsoever ye shall ask in MY (JESUS') name, that will I do, that the FATHER may be glorified in the SON. If ye shall ask anything in MY name, that will I do. If ye love ME, ye will keep MY commandments. And I will pray the FATHER, and HE shall give you another COMFORTER, that HE may be with you for ever, even the SPIRIT of truth: whom the world cannot receive; for it beholdeth HIM not, neither knoweth HIM: ye know HIM; for HE abideth with you, and shall be in you. I will not leave you desolate: I come unto you. Yet a little while, and the world beholdeth ME no more; but ye behold ME: because I live, ye shall live also. In that day ye shall know that I am in MY FATHER, and ye in ME, and I in you. He that hath MY commandments, and keepeth them, he it is that loveth ME: and he that loveth ME shall be loved of MY FATHER, and I will love him, and will manifest MYSELF unto him. Judas (not Iscariot) saith unto him, LORD, what is come to pass that THOU wilt manifest THYSELF unto us, and not unto the world? JESUS answered and said unto him, If a man love ME, he will keep MY word: and MY FATHER will love him, and WE will come unto him, and make OUR abode with him. He that loveth ME not keepeth not MY words: and the word which ye hear is not MINE, but the FATHER's

40

WHO sent ME. These things have I spoken unto you, while yet abiding with you. But the COMFORTER, even the HOLY SPIRIT, WHOM the FATHER will send in MY name, HE shall teach you all things, and bring to your remembrance all that I said unto you. Peace I leave with you; MY peace I give unto you: not as the world giveth, give I unto you. Let not your heart be troubled, neither let it be fearful."

John 16:5-11, (JESUS speaking) "But now I go unto HIM (GOD) that sent ME; and none of you asketh ME, Whither goest thou? But because I have spoken these things unto you, sorrow hath filled your heart. Nevertheless I tell you the truth: It is expedient for you that I go away; for if I go not away, the COMFORTER will not come unto you; but if I go, I will send HIM unto you. And HE, when HE is come, will convict the world in respect of sin, and of righteousness, and of judgment: of sin, because they believe not on ME; of righteousness, because I go to the FATHER, and ye behold ME no more; of judgment, because the prince of this world hath been judged."

2 Corinthians 4:7-18, "But we have this treasure in earthen vessels, that the exceeding greatness of the power may be of GOD, and not from ourselves; we are pressed on every side, yet not straitened; perplexed, yet not unto despair; pursued, yet not forsaken; smitten down, yet not destroyed; always bearing about in the body the dying of JESUS, that the life also of JESUS may be manifested in our body. For we who live are always delivered unto death for JESUS' sake, that the life also of JESUS may be manifested in our mortal flesh. So then death worketh in us, but life in you. But having the same spirit of faith, according to that which is written, I believed, and therefore did I speak; we also believe, and therefore also we speak; knowing that HE that raised up the LORD JESUS shall raise up us also with JESUS, and shall present us with you. For all things are for your sakes, that the grace, being multiplied through the many, may cause the thanksgiving to abound unto the glory of GOD. Wherefore we faint not; but though our outward man is decaying, yet our inward man is renewed day by day. For our light affliction, which is for the moment, worketh for us more and more exceedingly an eternal weight of glory; while we look not at the things which are seen, but at the things which are not seen: for the things which are seen are temporal; but the things which are not seen are eternal."

Ω

GOD desires me to be an ambassador of peace, and that is an achievement through humility. The truth is, my interactions with people are a reflection of my relationship with GOD. GOD is watching my interactions with others to see if I believe in HIM by my response to HIS WORD towards you. When I have leverage, and I concede it for what I believe benefits all involved is the greatest humble peace I can attain as JESUS states.

A

John 15:11-14, (JESUS speaking) "These things have I spoken unto you, that MY joy may be in you, and that your joy may be made full. This is MY commandment, that ye love one another, even as I have loved you. Greater love hath no man than this, that a man lay down his life for his friends. Ye are MY friends, if ye do the things which I command you."

Ω

Scripture is a composition of personal experiences with GOD, written by men inspired by GOD in truth. Being inspired by GOD means it is not whitewashed in order to convey a favorable point of view or disillusion the reader. It means GOD humbles himself to allow scripture to be exactly what it is...the truth, but I must search to find the principle HE is attempting to teach me. HE does not want *The Holy Bible* to be a simple read, so that I can simply mirror the words without thought or conscience.

Have I ever pushed too hard on family members because of something I believe, and they do not have the same belief? Yes. Have I had a predisposition before reading scripture, and after reading a scripture that pertains to that issue that I am right in every case? No, and later having read that scripture I had to realign my belief.

Will my experiences manipulate my belief of how I view GOD? Yes. GOD works like a well-managed corporation except HIS profit is love, and a corporation's profit is revenue. Both have to navigate each individual's issues to accomplish a purpose, delegate responsibilities, and produce positive results. Humility helps me respect people GOD put in authority, and I have to submit as long as instructions are lawful, even if those instructions may lead to death.

A

Matthew 3:1-15, "And in those days cometh John the Baptist, preaching in the wilderness of Judaea, saying, Repent ye; for the kingdom of heaven is at hand. For this is he that was spoken of through Isaiah the prophet, saying, The voice of one crying in the wilderness, Make ye ready the way of the LORD, Make HIS paths straight. Now John himself had his raiment of camel's hair, and a leathern girdle about his loins; and his food was locusts and wild honey. Then went out unto him Jerusalem, and all Judaea, and all the region round about the Jordan; and they were baptized of him in the river Jordan, confessing their sins. But when he saw many of the Pharisees and Sadducees coming to his baptism, he said unto them, Ye offspring of vipers, who warned you to flee from the wrath to come? Bring forth therefore fruit worthy of repentance: and think not to say within yourselves, We have Abraham to our father: for I say unto you, that GOD is able of these stones to raise up children unto Abraham. And even now the axe lieth at the root of the trees: every tree therefore that bringeth not forth good fruit is hewn down, and cast into the fire. I indeed baptize you in water unto repentance: but HE that cometh after me is mightier than I, whose shoes I am not worthy to bear: HE shall baptize you in the HOLY SPIRIT and in fire: WHOSE fan is in HIS hand, and HE will thoroughly cleanse HIS threshing-floor; and HE will gather HIS wheat into the garner, but the chaff HE will burn up with unquenchable fire. Then cometh JESUS from Galilee to the Jordan unto John, to be baptized of him. But John would have hindered HIM, saying, I have need to be baptized of THEE, and comest THOU to me? But JESUS answering said unto him, Suffer it now: for thus it becometh us to fulfil all righteousness. Then he suffereth HIM."

John 3:22-30, "After these things came JESUS and HIS disciples into the land of Judea; and there HE tarried with them, and baptized. And John also was baptizing in Enon near to Salim, because there was much water there: and they came, and were baptized. For John was not yet cast into prison. There arose therefore a questioning on the part of John's disciples with a Jew about purifying. And they came unto John, and said to him, Rabbi, HE that was with thee beyond the Jordan, to whom thou hast borne witness, behold, the same baptizeth, and all men come to HIM. John answered and said, A man can receive nothing, except it have been given him from heaven. Ye yourselves bear me witness, that I said, I am not the CHRIST, but, that I am sent before HIM. HE that hath the bride is the BRIDEGROOM: but the friend of the BRIDEGROOM, that standeth and heareth HIM, rejoiceth greatly because of the bridegroom's voice: this my joy therefore is made full. HE must increase, but I must decrease."

Matthew 14:1-12, "At that season Herod the tetrarch heard the report concerning JESUS, and said unto his servants, This is John the Baptist; he is risen from the dead; and therefore do these powers work in HIM. For Herod had laid hold on John, and bound him, and put him in prison for the sake of Herodias, his brother Philip's wife. For John said unto him, It is not lawful for thee to have her. And when he would have put him to death, he feared the multitude, because they counted him as a prophet. But when Herod's birthday came, the daughter of Herodias danced in the midst, and pleased Herod. Whereupon he promised with an oath to give her whatsoever she should ask. And she, being put forward by her mother, saith, Give me here on a platter the head of John the Baptist. And the king was grieved; but for the sake of his oaths, and of them that sat at meat with him, he commanded it to be given; and he sent and beheaded John in the prison. And his head was brought on a platter, and given to the damsel: and she brought it to her mother. And his disciples came, and took up the corpse, and buried him; and they went and told JESUS."

John 19:6-16, "When therefore the chief priests and the officers saw HIM (JESUS), they cried out, saying, Crucify HIM, crucify HIM! Pilate saith unto them, Take HIM yourselves, and crucify HIM: for I find no crime in HIM. The Jews answered him, We have a law, and by that law HE ought to die, because HE made HIMSELF the SON of GOD. When Pilate therefore heard this saying, he was the more afraid; and he entered into the Praetorium again, and saith unto JESUS, Whence art thou? But JESUS gave him no answer. Pilate therefore saith unto HIM, Speakest THOU not unto me? Knowest THOU not that I have power to release THEE, and have power to crucify THEE? JESUS answered him, Thou wouldest have no power against ME, except it were given thee from above: therefore he that delivered ME unto thee hath greater sin. Upon this Pilate sought to release HIM: but the Jews cried out, saying, If thou release this MAN, thou art not Caesar's friend: every one that maketh himself a king speaketh against Caesar. When Pilate therefore heard these words, he brought JESUS out, and sat down on the judgment-seat at a place called The Pavement, but in Hebrew, Gabbatha. Now it was the Preparation of the passover: it was about the sixth hour. And he saith unto the Jews, Behold, your KING! They therefore cried out, Away with HIM, away with HIM crucify HIM! Pilate saith unto them, Shall I crucify your KING? The chief priests answered, We have no king but Caesar. Then therefore he delivered HIM unto them to be crucified."

Ω

JESUS yielded to man's authority, and humbled HIMSELF to obedience to both GOD and man. Peace is maintained with consistency, and humility is the sweet savor of service. If GOD in the form of JESUS maintained peace through humility to earthly authority, then by HIS SPIRIT, HIS example empowers me to conform to be like HIM.

RIGHTEOUSNESS

Chapter 6

What is righteousness? Each individual person has their own ideas of what is the right thing to do, and that is why a standard of "righteousness" is established in written law. *The Pentateuch* is the first five books of *The Holy Bible*, and in *The New Testament* it is referred to as "The Law" or "The Law of Moses." As a Christian, I must understand that my actions are to be governed by the language in those five books. Both *Exodus* and *Deuteronomy* have "The Ten Commandments," and when tempted by the devil, JESUS invalidated those temptations with quotes from *Deuteronomy*, which is part of "The Law."

A

Luke 4:1-13, "And JESUS, full of the HOLY SPIRIT, returned from the Jordan, and was led in the SPIRIT in the wilderness during forty days, being tempted of the devil. And HE did eat nothing in those days: and when they were completed, HE hungered. And the devil said unto HIM, if THOU art the SON of GOD, command this stone that it become bread. And JESUS answered unto him, It is written, Man shall not live by bread alone. And he led HIM up, and showed HIM all the kingdoms of the world in a moment of time. And the devil said unto HIM, To THEE will I give all this authority, and the glory of them: for it hath been delivered unto me; and to whomsoever I will I give it. If THOU therefore wilt worship before me, it shall all be THINE. And JESUS answered and said unto him, It is written, Thou shalt worship the LORD thy GOD, and HIM only shalt thou serve. And he led HIM to Jerusalem, and set HIM on the pinnacle of the temple, and said unto HIM, If THOU art the SON of GOD, cast THYSELF down from hence: for it is written, HE shall give HIS angels charge concerning THEE, to guard THEE: and, On their hands they shall bear THEE up, Lest haply THOU dash THY foot against a stone. And JESUS answering said unto him, It is said, Thou shalt not make trial of the LORD thy GOD. And when the devil had completed every temptation, he departed from HIM for a season."

Deuteronomy 8:1-3, "All the commandment which I command thee this day shall ye observe to do, that ye may live, and multiply, and go in and possess the land which JEHOVAH sware unto your fathers. And thou shalt remember all the way which JEHOVAH thy GOD hath led thee these forty years in the wilderness, that HE might humble thee, to prove thee, to know what was in thy heart, whether thou wouldest keep HIS commandments, or not. And HE humbled thee, and suffered thee to hunger, and fed thee with manna, which thou knewest not, neither did thy fathers know; that HE might make thee know that man doth not live by bread only, but by everything that proceedeth out of the mouth of JEHOVAH doth man live."

Deuteronomy 6:13-17, "Thou shalt fear JEHOVAH thy GOD; and HIM shalt thou serve, and shalt swear by HIS name. Ye shall not go after other gods, of the gods of the peoples that are round about you; for JEHOVAH thy GOD in the midst of thee is a jealous GOD; lest the anger of JEHOVAH thy GOD be kindled against thee, and he destroy thee from off the face of the earth. Ye shall not tempt JEHOVAH your GOD, as ye tempted him in Massah. Ye shall diligently keep the commandments of JEHOVAH your GOD, and HIS testimonies, and HIS statutes, which HE hath commanded thee."

Ω

Righteousness is to be viewed from GOD's point of view. That is a simple thought, but it is the intent of the thought discovers righteousness. Is turning a stone into bread a sin? Is being a world leader a sin? Is worshipping another god a sin? Is testing GOD a sin? Temptation is a deliberate attempt by the devil to void GOD's word, and confuse me, so that I become uncertain about GOD's instructions.

A

Genesis 2:16-17, "And JEHOVAH GOD commanded the man, saying, Of every tree of the garden thou mayest freely eat: but of the tree of the knowledge of good and evil, thou shalt not eat of it: for in the day that thou eatest thereof thou shalt surely die."

Genesis 3:1-7, "Now the serpent was more subtle than any beast of the field which JEHOVAH GOD had made. And he said unto the woman, Yea, hath GOD said, Ye shall not eat of any tree of the garden? And the woman said unto the serpent, Of the fruit of the trees of the garden we may eat: but of the fruit of the tree which is in the midst of the garden, GOD hath said, Ye shall not eat of it, neither shall ye touch it, lest ye die. And the serpent said unto the woman, Ye shall not surely die: for GOD doth know that in the day ye eat thereof, then your eyes shall be opened, and ye shall be as GOD, knowing good and evil. And when the woman saw that the tree was good for food, and that it was a delight to the eyes, and that the tree was to be desired to make one wise, she took of the fruit thereof, and did eat; and she gave also unto her husband with her, and he did eat. And the eyes of them both were opened, and they knew that they were naked; and they sewed fig-leaves together, and made themselves aprons."

Ω

How does GOD view righteousness? Righteousness is simply believing HIM. *The Holy Bible* composes HIS WORD on how I am to govern myself. If I act in accordance to HIS WORD, then what I am revealing about myself is that I believe HIS WORD is truth.

A

Genesis 15:1-6, "After these things the word of JEHOVAH came unto Abram in a vision, saying, Fear not, Abram: I am thy SHIELD, and thy EXCEEDING GREAT REWARD. And Abram said, O LORD JEHOVAH, what wilt THOU give me, seeing I go childless, and he that shall be possessor of my house is Eliezer of Damascus?

And Abram said, Behold, to me THOU hast given no seed: and, lo, one born in my house is mine heir. And, behold, the WORD of JEHOVAH came unto him, saying, This man shall not be thine heir; But he that shall come forth out of thine own bowels shall be thine heir. And HE brought him forth abroad, and said, Look now toward heaven, and number the stars, if thou be able to number them: and he said unto him, So shall thy seed be. And he believed in JEHOVAH; and HE reckoned it to him for righteousness."

Ω

Abram initiated intimacy with his wife, Sarai, and acted upon GOD's instruction with the practical knowledge that children are conceived through intercourse. After the deliverance of children of Israel from Egypt, they repeatedly complained about their circumstances. Thereby provoked GOD's anger because of their constant complaints.

HE had enough when their fear prevented them from entering "The Promise Land," but HE rewarded Caleb and Joshua for believing HIM. HE wanted them to realize that HE brought them out of Egypt for the purpose of their benefit not destruction, and in turn HE would be magnified in glory, so that others would acknowledge the evidence of HIS majesty in order to come to HIM.

A

Numbers 13:17-14:30, "And Moses sent them to spy out the land of Canaan, and said unto them, Get you up this way by the South, and go up into the hill-country: and see the land, what it is; and the people that dwell therein, whether they are strong or weak, whether they are few or many; and what the land is that they dwell in, whether it is good or bad; and what cities they are that they dwell in, whether in camps, or in strongholds; and what the land is, whether it is fat or lean, whether there is wood therein, or not. And be ye of good courage, and bring of the fruit of the land. Now the time was the time of the first-ripe grapes. So they went up, and spied out the land from the wilderness of Zin unto Rehob, to the entrance of Hamath. And they went up by the South, and came unto Hebron; and Ahiman, Sheshai, and Talmai, the children of Anak, were there. (Now Hebron was built seven years before Zoan in Egypt.) And they came unto the valley of Eshcol, and cut down from thence a branch with one cluster of grapes, and they bare it upon a staff between two; they brought also of the pomegranates, and of the figs. That place was called the valley of Eshcol, because of the cluster which the children of Israel cut down from thence. And they returned from spying out the land at the end of forty days. And they went and came to Moses, and to Aaron, and to all the congregation of the children of Israel, unto the wilderness of Paran, to Kadesh; and brought back word unto them, and unto all the congregation, and showed them the fruit of the land. And they told him, and said, We came unto the land whither thou sentest us; and surely it floweth with milk and honey; and this is the fruit of it. Howbeit the people that dwell in the land are strong, and the cities are fortified, and very great: and moreover we saw the children of Anak there. Amalek dwelleth in the land of the South: and the Hittite, and the Jebusite, and the Amorite, dwell in the hill-country; and the Canaanite dwelleth by the sea, and along by the side of the Jordan. And Caleb stilled the people before Moses, and said, Let us go up at once, and possess it; for we are well able to overcome it. But the men that went up with him said, We are not able to go up against the people; for they are stronger than we. And they brought up an evil report of the land which they had spied out unto the children of Israel, saying, The land, through which we have gone to spy it out, is a land that eateth up the inhabitants thereof; and all the people that we saw in it are men of great stature. And there we saw the Nephilim, the sons of Anak, who come of the Nephilim: and we were in our own sight as grasshoppers, and so we were in their sight. And all the congregation lifted up their voice, and cried; and the people wept that night. And all the children of Israel murmured against Moses and against Aaron: and the whole congregation said unto them, Would that we had died in the land of Egypt! or would that we had died in this wilderness! And wherefore doth JEHOVAH bring us unto this land, to fall by the sword? Our wives and our little ones will be a prey: were it not better for us to return into Egypt? And they said one to another, Let us make a captain, and let us return into Egypt. Then Moses and Aaron fell on their faces before all the assembly of the congregation of the children of Israel. And Joshua the son of Nun and Caleb the son of Jephunneh, who were of them that spied out the land, rent their clothes: and they spake unto all the congregation of the children of Israel, saying, The land, which we passed through to spy it out, is an exceeding good land. If JEHOVAH delight in us, then HE will bring us into this land, and give it unto us; a land which floweth with milk and honey. Only rebel not against JEHOVAH, neither fear ye the people of the land; for they are bread for us: their defence is removed from over them, and JEHOVAH is with us: fear them not. But all the congregation bade stone them with stones. And the glory of JEHOVAH appeared in the tent of meeting unto all the children of Israel. And JEHOVAH said unto Moses, How long will this people despise ME? and how long will they not believe in ME, for all the signs which I have wrought among them? I will smite them with the pestilence, and dis-inherit them, and will make of thee a nation greater and mightier than they. And Moses said unto JEHOVAH, Then the Egyptians will hear it; for THOU broughtest up this people in THY might from among them; and they will tell it to the inhabitants of this land. They have heard that THOU JEHOVAH art in the midst of this people; for THOU JEHOVAH art seen face to face, and thy cloud standeth over them, and THOU goest before them, in a pillar of cloud by day, and in a pillar of fire by night. Now if THOU shalt kill this people as one man, then the nations which have heard the fame of THEE will speak, saying, Because JEHOVAH was not able to bring this people into the land which HE sware unto them, therefore HE hath slain them in the wilderness. And now, I pray THEE, let the power of the LORD be great, according as THOU hast spoken, saying, JEHOVAH is slow to anger, and abundant in lovingkindness, forgiving iniquity and trans-gression; and that will by no means clear the guilty, visiting the iniq-uity of the fathers upon the children, upon the third and upon the fourth generation. Pardon, I pray THEE, the iniquity of this people according unto the greatness of THY lovingkindness, and according as THOU hast forgiven this people, from Egypt even until now. And

JEHOVAH said, I have pardoned according to thy word: but in very deed, as I live, and as all the earth shall be filled with the glory of JEHOVAH; because all those men that have seen MY glory, and MY signs, which I wrought in Egypt and in the wilderness, yet have tempted ME these ten times, and have not hearkened to MY voice; surely they shall not see the land which I sware unto their fathers, neither shall any of them that despised ME see it: but MY servant Caleb, because he had another spirit with him, and hath followed ME fully, him will I bring into the land whereinto he went; and his seed shall possess it. Now the Amalekite and the Canaanite dwell in the valley: to-morrow turn ye, and get you into the wilderness by the way to the Red Sea. And JEHOVAH spake unto Moses and unto Aaron, saying, How long shall I bear with this evil congregation, that murmur against ME? I have heard the murmurings of the children of Israel, which they murmur against ME. Say unto them, As I live, saith JEHOVAH, surely as ye have spoken in MINE ears, so will I do to you: your dead bodies shall fall in this wilderness; and all that were numbered of you, according to your whole number, from twenty years old and upward, that have murmured against ME, surely ye shall not come into the land, concerning which I sware that I would make you dwell therein, save Caleb the son of Jephunneh, and Joshua the son of Nun."

Ω

Gideon believed GOD by reducing his army before going to war. GOD wanted Gideon to understand that HE makes deliverance possible. Now Gideon acted on this precept from *Deuteronomy*, whether he knew it or not.

A

Judges 7:1-7, "Then Jerubbaal, who is Gideon, and all the people that were with him, rose up early, and encamped beside the spring of Harod: and the camp of Midian was on the north side of them, by the hill of Moreh, in the valley. And JEHOVAH said unto Gideon, The people that are with thee are too many for me to give the Midianites into their hand, lest Israel vaunt themselves against ME, saying, Mine own hand hath saved me. Now therefore proclaim in the ears of the people, saying, Whosoever is fearful and trembling, let him return and depart from mount Gilead. And there returned of the people twenty and two thousand; and there remained ten thousand. And JEHOVAH said unto Gideon, The people are yet too many; bring them down unto the water, and I will try them for thee there: and it shall be, that of whom I say unto thee, This shall go with thee, the same shall go with thee; and of whomsoever I say unto thee, This shall not go with thee, the same shall not go. So he brought down the people unto the water: and JEHOVAH said unto Gideon, Every one that lappeth of the water with his tongue, as a dog lappeth, him shalt thou set by himself; likewise every one that boweth down upon his knees to drink. And the number of them that lapped, putting their hand to their mouth, was three hundred men: but all the rest of the people bowed down upon their knees to drink water. And JEHOVAH said unto Gideon, By the three hundred men that lapped will I save you, and deliver the Midianites into thy hand; and let all the people go every man unto his place."

Deuteronomy 20:2-8, "And it shall be, when ye draw nigh unto the battle, that the priest shall approach and speak unto the people, and shall say unto them, Hear, O Israel, ye draw nigh this day unto battle against your enemies: let not your heart faint; fear not, nor tremble, neither be ye affrighted at them; for JEHOVAH your GOD is HE that goeth with you, to fight for you against your enemies, to save you. And the officers shall speak unto the people, saying, What man is there that hath built a new house, and hath not dedicated it? let him go and return to his house, lest he die in the battle, and another man dedicate it. And what man is there that hath planted a vineyard, and hath not used the fruit thereof? let him go and return unto his house, lest he die in the battle, and another man use the fruit thereof. And what man is there that hath betrothed a wife, and hath not taken her? let him go and return unto his house, lest he die in the battle, and another man take her. And the officers shall speak further unto the people, and they shall say, What man is there that is fearful and faint-hearted? let him go and return unto his house, lest his brethren's heart melt as his heart."

Ω

Boaz plans a course of action in order to marry Ruth. He had a plan motivated by righteous as defined by "The Law." He took matters into his own hands, but he did not conjure up his own ideas to implement a resolution. He simply did what "The Law" required.

A

Ruth 3:7-13, "And when Boaz had eaten and drunk, and his heart was merry, he went to lie down at the end of the heap of grain: and she (Ruth) came softly, and uncovered his feet, and laid her down. And it came to pass at midnight, that the man was afraid, and turned himself; and, behold, a woman lay at his feet. And he said, Who art thou? And she answered, I am Ruth thy handmaid: spread therefore thy skirt over thy handmaid; for thou art a near kinsman. And he said, Blessed be thou of JEHOVAH, my daughter: thou hast showed more kindness in the latter end than at the beginning, inasmuch as thou followedst not young men, whether poor or rich. And now, my daughter, fear not; I will do to thee all that thou sayest; for all the city of my people doth know that thou art a worthy woman. And now it is true that I am a near kinsman; howbeit there is a kinsman nearer than I. Tarry this night, and it shall be in the morning, that if he will perform unto thee the part of a kinsman, well; let him do the kinsman's part: but if he will not do the part of a kinsman to thee, then will I do the part of a kinsman to thee, as JEHOVAH liveth: lie down until the morning."

Ruth 4:1-13, "Now Boaz went up to the gate, and sat him down there: and, behold, the near kinsman of whom Boaz spake came by; unto

whom he said, Ho, such a one! turn aside, sit down here. And he turned aside, and sat down. And he took ten men of the elders of the city,
and said, Sit ye down here. And they sat down. And he said unto the
near kinsman, Naomi, that is come again out of the country of Moab,
selleth the parcel of land, which was our brother Elimelech's: And I
thought to disclose it unto thee, saying, Buy it before them that sit
here, and before the elders of my people. If thou wilt redeem it, redeem it: but if thou wilt not redeem it, then tell me, that I may know;
for there is none to redeem it besides thee; and I am after thee. And
he said, I will redeem it. Then said Boaz, What day thou buyest the
field of the hand of Naomi, thou must buy it also of Ruth the Moabitess, the wife of the dead, to raise up the name of the dead upon his
inheritance. And the near kinsman said, I cannot redeem it for myself,
lest I mar mine own inheritance: take thou my right of redemption on
thee; for I cannot redeem it. Now this was the custom in former time
in Israel concerning redeeming and concerning exchanging, to confirm all things: a man drew off his shoe, and gave it to his neighbor;
and this was the manner of attestation in Israel. So the near kinsman
said unto Boaz, Buy it for thyself. And he drew off his shoe. And
Boaz said unto the elders, and unto all the people, Ye are witnesses
this day, that I have bought all that was Elimelech's, and all that was
Chilion's and Mahlon's, of the hand of Naomi. Moreover Ruth the
Moabitess, the wife of Mahlon, have I purchased to be my wife, to
raise up the name of the dead upon his inheritance, that the name of
the dead be not cut off from among his brethren, and from the gate of
his place: ye are witnesses this day. And all the people that were in
the gate, and the elders, said, We are witnesses. JEHOVAH make the
woman that is come into thy house like Rachel and like Leah, which
two did build the house of Israel: and do thou worthily in Ephrathah,
and be famous in Bethlehem: and let thy house be like the house of
Perez, whom Tamar bare unto Judah, of the seed which JEHOVAH
shall give thee of this young woman. So Boaz took Ruth, and she
became his wife; and he went in unto her, and JEHOVAH gave her
conception, and she bare a son."

Deuteronomy 25:5-10, "If brethren dwell together, and one of them die, and have no son, the wife of the dead shall not be married without unto a stranger: her husband's brother shall go in unto her, and take her to him to wife, and perform the duty of a husband's brother unto her. And it shall be, that the first-born that she beareth shall succeed in the name of his brother that is dead, that his name be not blotted out of Israel. And if the man like not to take his brother's wife, then his brother's wife shall go up to the gate unto the elders, and say, My husband's brother refuseth to raise up unto his brother a name in Israel; he will not perform the duty of a husband's brother unto me. Then the elders of his city shall call him, and speak unto him: and if he stand, and say, I like not to take her; then shall his brother's wife come unto him in the presence of the elders, and loose his shoe from off his foot, and spit in his face; and she shall answer and say, So shall it be done unto the man that doth not build up his brother's house. And his name shall be called in Israel, The house of him that hath his shoe loosed."

Ω

The Old Testament is still the foundational basis of righteousness, for *The New Testament*. Most Christians do not recognize the concept because *The Old Testament* is perceived as inferior. Fundamental doctrine has to have a foundation to build, and JESUS affirms it. The Canaanite woman prompted JESUS to act from having a concept from *The Old Testament*. Dogs are entitled to scraps, and her knowledge of scripture as well as identifying herself as a dog saved her child.

A

Matthew 5:17-20, (JESUS speaking) "Think not that I came to destroy the law or the prophets: I came not to destroy, but to fulfil. For verily I say unto you, Till heaven and earth pass away, one jot or one tittle shall in no wise pass away from the law, till all things be accomplished. Whosoever therefore shall break one of these least commandments, and shall teach men so, shall be called least in the kingdom of heaven: but whosoever shall do and teach them, he shall be called great in the kingdom of heaven. For I say unto you, that except your righteousness shall exceed the righteousness of the scribes and Pharisees, ye shall in no wise enter into the kingdom of heaven."

Matthew 15:22-28, "And behold, a Canaanitish woman came out from those borders, and cried, saying, Have mercy on me, O LORD, thou SON of David; my daughter is grievously vexed with a demon. But HE (JESUS) answered her not a word. And HIS disciples came and besought HIM, saying, Send her away; for she crieth after us. But HE answered and said, I was not sent but unto the lost sheep of the house of Israel. But she came and worshipped HIM, saying, LORD, help me. And HE answered and said, It is not meet to take the children's bread and cast it to the dogs. But she said, Yea, LORD: for even the dogs eat of the crumbs which fall from their masters' table. Then JESUS answered and said unto her, O woman, great is thy faith: be it done unto thee even as thou wilt. And her daughter was healed from that hour."

Exodus 22:31, (GOD speaking) "And ye shall be holy men unto ME: therefore ye shall not eat any flesh that is torn of beasts in the field; ye shall cast it to the dogs."

Psalms 147:7-9, "Sing unto JEHOVAH with thanksgiving; Sing praises upon the harp unto our GOD, Who covereth the heavens with clouds, Who prepareth rain for the earth, Who maketh grass to grow upon the mountains. HE giveth to the beast his food, And to the young ravens which cry."

Proverbs 12:10, "A righteous man regardeth the life of his beast; But the tender mercies of the wicked are cruel."

Ω

Zacchæus responded to the call of JESUS. He made a decla-
ration of his faith based from *The Old Testament,* and then exceeds
what "The Law" required by also giving half of his goods to the poor.
My opinion is insignificant without reference to HIS WORD, and my
opinion without HIS WORD hinders the HOLY SPIRIT educating
me. *The Holy Bible* is the map to teach me how to respond to life's
issues. I can pray about an issue, but I absolutely must submit to HIS
process of judgment.

A

Luke 19:1-10, "And HE (JESUS) entered and was passing through
Jericho. And behold, a man called by name Zacchaeus; and he was a
chief, and he was rich. And he sought to see JESUS WHO HE was;
and could not for the crowd, because he was little of stature. And he
ran on before, and climbed up into a sycomore tree to see HIM: for
HE was to pass that way. And when JESUS came to the place, HE
looked up, and said unto him, Zacchaeus, make haste, and come
down; for to-day I must abide at thy house. And he made haste, and
came down, and received HIM joyfully. And when they saw it, they
all murmured, saying, HE is gone in to lodge with a man that is a
sinner. And Zacchaeus stood, and said unto the LORD, Behold,
LORD, the half of my goods I give to the poor; and if I have wrong-
fully exacted aught of any man, I restore fourfold. And JESUS said
unto him, To-day is salvation come to this house, forasmuch as he
also is a son of Abraham. For the SON of man came to seek and to
save that which was lost."

Exodus 22:1, "If a man shall steal an ox, or a sheep, and kill it, or sell
it; he shall pay five oxen for an ox, and four sheep for a sheep."

Ω

The Holy Bible shows both correct and incorrect responses, and *The Pentateuch* are landmarks on life's map. Trying to understand GOD's righteousness without the boundary of *The Pentateuch* is telling a story out of context like having car without wheels. Righteousness is seeking the values of GOD's desire, and yielding my will to accomplish HIS values.

A

Proverbs 15:9, "The way of the wicked is an abomination to JEHOVAH; But HE loveth him that followeth after righteousness."

Ω

Start simple, loving my wife as CHRIST loves the Church, and teach my children about GOD. Find ways to live in peace with people. Do my job as instructed in accordance to the law and training. Expressing the Gospel though word and deed. These are the fundamentals as GOD opens doors of opportunity.

A

Deuteronomy 30:9-14, "And JEHOVAH thy GOD will make thee plenteous in all the work of thy hand, in the fruit of thy body, and in the fruit of thy cattle, and in the fruit of thy ground, for good: for JEHOVAH will again rejoice over thee for good, as HE rejoiced over thy fathers; if thou shalt obey the voice of JEHOVAH thy GOD, to keep HIS commandments and HIS statutes which are written in this book of the law; if thou turn unto JEHOVAH thy GOD with all thy heart, and with all thy soul. For this commandment which I command thee this day, it is not too hard for thee, neither is it far off. It is not in heaven, that thou shouldest say, Who shall go up for us to heaven, and bring it unto us, and make us to hear it, that we may do it? Neither is it beyond the sea, that thou shouldest say, Who shall go over the sea for us, and bring it unto us, and make us to hear it, that we may do it? But the WORD is very nigh unto thee, in thy mouth, and in thy heart, that thou mayest do it."

Ω

Moses declares that I am guilty if I do not seek GOD's WORD, and Paul reiterates it. In order to have a better understanding of the setting of *The New Testament*, I need an education of *The Old Testament*, and who better to instruct than Jewish teachers. The nuances of their culture may cause me to misrepresent the meaning of vocabulary or gesture, if I am only instructed by gentiles, who are partial to *The New Testament*, then I am pliable in my education because I do not have the foundational principles from *The Old Testament*, and therefore easily manipulated by the will of men, who are innovative and ambitious.

A

Romans 10:4-10, "For CHRIST is the end of the law unto righteousness to every one that believeth. For Moses writeth that the man that doeth the righteousness which is of the law shall live thereby. But the righteousness which is of faith saith thus, Say not in thy heart, Who shall ascend into heaven? (that is, to bring CHRIST down:) or, Who shall descend into the abyss? (That is, to bring CHRIST up from the dead.) But what saith it? The WORD is nigh thee, in thy mouth, and in thy heart: that is, the WORD of faith, which we preach: because if thou shalt confess with thy mouth JESUS as LORD, and shalt believe in thy heart that GOD raised HIM from the dead, thou shalt be saved: for with the heart man believeth unto righteousness; and with the mouth confession is made unto salvation."

Zechariah 8:20-23, "Thus saith JEHOVAH of hosts: It shall yet come to pass, that there shall come peoples, and the inhabitants of many cities; and the inhabitants of one city shall go to another, saying, Let us go speedily to entreat the favor of JEHOVAH, and to seek

JEHOVAH of hosts: I will go also. Yea, many peoples and strong nations shall come to seek JEHOVAH of hosts in Jerusalem, and to entreat the favor of JEHOVAH. Thus saith JEHOVAH of hosts: In those days it shall come to pass, that ten men shall take hold, out of all the languages of the nations, they shall take hold of the skirt of him that is a Jew, saying, We will go with you, for we have heard that GOD is with you."

Hosea 4:6, "MY people are destroyed for lack of knowledge: because thou hast rejected knowledge, I will also reject thee, that thou shalt be no priest to ME: seeing thou hast forgotten the law of thy GOD, I also will forget thy children."

Ω

That verse provides insight into the hazards of the lack of knowledge, so a legalist believes a person not seeking knowledge of GOD is liable for their circumstances even if the legalist puts them in those circumstances. The legalist is unencumbered from my ignorance, and believes he has a right to take advantage of me since knowledge is my responsibility. Legalist do not have to inform me of GOD's righteousness, so as to improve my life's benefits.

The Pentateuch states my rights, my family's rights, my neighbor's rights, the king's rights, employer's rights, employee's rights, and foreigner's rights. It maps how to conduct my behavior, and how others are to conduct themselves with me. Now JESUS instructs me to meditate on the application of *The Old Testament* literature.

A

Matthew 9:4-8, "And JESUS knowing their thoughts said, Wherefore think ye evil in your hearts? For which is easier, to say, Thy sins are forgiven; or to say, Arise, and walk? But that ye may know that the SON of man hath authority on earth to forgive sins (then saith he to

62

the sick of the palsy), Arise, and take up thy bed, and go up unto thy house. And he arose, and departed to his house. But when the multitudes saw it, they were afraid, and glorified GOD, who had given such authority unto men."

Luke 6:6-11, "And it came to pass on another sabbath, that HE (JESUS) entered into the synagogue and taught: and there was a man there, and his right hand was withered. And the scribes and the Pharisees watched HIM, whether HE would heal on the sabbath; that they might find how to accuse HIM. But HE knew their thoughts; and HE said to the man that had his hand withered, Rise up, and stand forth in the midst. And he arose and stood forth. And JESUS said unto them, I ask you, Is it lawful on the sabbath to do good, or to do harm? to save a life, or to destroy it? And HE looked round about on them all, and said unto him, Stretch forth thy hand. And he did so: and his hand was restored. But they were filled with madness; and communed one with another what they might do to JESUS."

Ω

Unfortunately, manipulation of legal standard is precedent by redefining vocabulary and language. This is done all the time in legal matters. Such as in the matter of marriage and divorce according to "The Law of Moses." Initially Moses states circumstances for when a husband cannot divorce his wife. Two chapters later the terms for divorce changed.

A

Deuteronomy 22:13-19, "If any man take a wife, and go in unto her, and hate her, and lay shameful things to her charge, and bring up an evil name upon her, and say, I took this woman, and when I came nigh to her, I found not in her the tokens of virginity; then shall the father of the damsel, and her mother, take and bring forth the tokens of the damsel's virginity unto the elders of the city in the gate; and the damsel's father shall say unto the elders, I gave my daughter unto this man to wife, and he hateth her; and, lo, he hath laid shameful things to her charge, saying, I found not in thy daughter the tokens of virginity; and yet these are the tokens of my daughter's virginity. And they shall spread the garment before the elders of the city. And the elders of that city shall take the man and chastise him; and they shall fine him a hundred shekels of silver, and give them unto the father of the damsel, because he hath brought up an evil name upon a virgin of Israel: and she shall be his wife; he may not put her away all his days."

Deuteronomy 22:28-29, "If a man find a damsel that is a virgin, that is not betrothed, and lay hold on her, and lie with her, and they be found; then the man that lay with her shall give unto the damsel's father fifty shekels of silver, and she shall be his wife, because he hath humbled her; he may not put her away all his days."

Deuteronomy 24:1, "When a man taketh a wife, and marrieth her, then it shall be, if she find no favor in his eyes, because he hath found some unseemly thing in her, that he shall write her a bill of divorcement, and give it in her hand, and send her out of his house."

Ω

Then JESUS states the reason Moses allowed the language to change because of the will of the people. Basically, Moses made a political calculation because men were rebelling against this law as he was trying to keep a burgeoning nation intact. JESUS is not hindered by such encumbrances, so HE informs me that I have to change, not HIM.

A

Matthew 19:3-8, "And there came unto HIM (JESUS) Pharisees, trying HIM, and saying, Is it lawful for a man to put away his wife for every cause? And HE answered and said, Have ye not read, that HE

WHO made them from the beginning made them male and female, and said, For this cause shall a man leave his father and mother, and shall cleave to his wife; and the two shall become one flesh? So that they are no more two, but one flesh. What therefore GOD hath joined together, let not man put asunder. They say unto HIM, Why then did Moses command to give a bill of divorcement, and to put her away? HE saith unto them, Moses for your hardness of heart suffered you to put away your wives: but from the beginning it hath not been so."

Ω

Another example, is throughout "The Law of Moses" the terms of conduct with a "neighbor" are detailed. "The Law" obligates fair and legal treatment to one another. The language is necessary to maintain peace and order in society.

A

Exodus 20:16-17, "Thou shalt not bear false witness against thy neighbor. Thou shalt not covet thy neighbor's house, thou shalt not covet thy neighbor's wife, nor his man-servant, nor his maid-servant, nor his ox, nor his ass, nor anything that is thy neighbor's."

Exodus 22:7-9, "If a man shall deliver unto his neighbor money or stuff to keep, and it be stolen out of the man's house; if the thief be found, he shall pay double. If the thief be not found, then the master of the house shall come near unto GOD, to see whether he have not put his hand unto his neighbor's goods. For every matter of trespass, whether it be for ox, for ass, for sheep, for raiment, or for any manner of lost thing, whereof one saith, This is it, the cause of both parties shall come before GOD; he whom GOD shall condemn shall pay double unto his neighbor."

Exodus 22:26-27, "If thou at all take thy neighbor's garment to pledge, thou shalt restore it unto him before the sun goeth down: for that is his only covering, it is his garment for his skin: wherein shall he sleep? And it shall come to pass, when he crieth unto ME, that I will hear; for I am gracious."

Leviticus 19:13-18, "Thou shalt not oppress thy neighbor, nor rob him: the wages of a hired servant shall not abide with thee all night until the morning. Thou shalt not curse the deaf, nor put a stumbling-block before the blind; but thou shalt fear thy GOD: I am JEHOVAH. Ye shall do no unrighteousness in judgment: thou shalt not respect the person of the poor, nor honor the person of the mighty; but in righteousness shalt thou judge thy neighbor. Thou shalt not go up and down as a talebearer among thy people: neither shalt thou stand against the blood of thy neighbor: I am JEHOVAH. Thou shalt not hate thy brother in thy heart: thou shalt surely rebuke thy neighbor, and not bear sin because of him. Thou shalt not take vengeance, nor bear any grudge against the children of thy people; but thou shalt love thy neighbor as thyself: I am JEHOVAH."

Deuteronomy 19:14, "Thou shalt not remove thy neighbor's land-mark, which they of old time have set, in thine inheritance which thou shalt inherit, in the land that JEHOVAH thy GOD giveth thee to possess it."

Ω

JESUS has a dialogue with a lawyer concerning the definition of the word "neighbor." Looking for a loophole, the lawyer asks JESUS to define the word "neighbor" because if the definitions more concise, then the lawyer will innovate in order to take advantage of those who are not protected by the legal definition of "neighbor." JESUS tells the Parable of the Good Samaritan, and gets the lawyer to confess who is the neighbor, so that the lawyer becomes accountable by his own words. Does that mean a person has to have mercy on me to be my neighbor? No, the parable is informing the lawyer that the one group of people, Samaritans, who were generally hated for racial and religious differences, are still entitled neighbors.

A

Luke 10:25-37, "And behold, a certain lawyer stood up and made trial of HIM (JESUS), saying, TEACHER, what shall I do to inherit eternal life? And HE said unto him, What is written in the law? how readest thou? And he answering said, Thou shalt love the LORD thy GOD with all thy heart, and with all thy soul, and with all thy strength, and with all thy mind; and thy neighbor as thyself. And HE said unto him, Thou hast answered right: this do, and thou shalt live. But he, desiring to justify himself, said unto JESUS, And who is my neighbor? JESUS made answer and said, A certain man was going down from Jerusalem to Jericho; and he fell among robbers, who both stripped him and beat him, and departed, leaving him half dead. And by chance a certain priest was going down that way: and when he saw him, he passed by on the other side. And in like manner a Levite also, when he came to the place, and saw him, passed by on the other side. But a certain Samaritan, as he journeyed, came where he was: and when he saw him, he was moved with compassion, and came to him, and bound up his wounds, pouring on them oil and wine; and he set him on his own beast, and brought him to an inn, and took care of him. And on the morrow he took out two shillings, and gave them to the host, and said, Take care of him; and whatsoever thou spendest more, I, when I come back again, will repay thee. Which of these three, thinkest thou, proved neighbor unto him that fell among the robbers? And he said, He that showed mercy on him. And JESUS said unto him, Go, and do thou likewise."

Ω

GOD's view is not corruptible by my prejudice, and HE judges me according to how I treat any and every person. *The Penta-*

teuch is part of the map of instructions on how GOD views the righteous acts that I am chosen to reenact in my living, but JESUS desires me to surpass "The Law" with love. Love is multiplied righteousness. From a gracious heart, it simply gives more than what is required.

A

Matthew 5:20-24, (JESUS speaking) "For I say unto you, that except your righteousness shall exceed the righteousness of the scribes and Pharisees, ye shall in no wise enter into the kingdom of heaven. Ye have heard that it was said to them of old time, Thou shalt not kill; and whosoever shall kill shall be in danger of the judgment: but I say unto you, that every one who is angry with his brother shall be in danger of the judgment; and whosoever shall say to his brother, Raca, shall be in danger of the council; and whosoever shall say, Thou fool, shall be in danger of the hell of fire. If therefore thou art offering thy gift at the altar, and there rememberest that thy brother hath aught against thee, leave there thy gift before the altar, and go thy way, first be reconciled to thy brother, and then come and offer thy gift."

Matthew 5:27-28, (JESUS speaking) "Ye have heard that it was said, Thou shalt not commit adultery: but I say unto you, that every one that looketh on a woman to lust after her hath committed adultery with her already in his heart."

Matthew 5:31-48, (JESUS speaking) "It was said also, Whosoever shall put away his wife, let him give her a writing of divorcement: but I say unto you, that every one that putteth away his wife, saving for the cause of fornication, maketh her an adulteress: and whosoever shall marry her when she is put away committeth adultery. Again, ye have heard that it was said to them of old time, Thou shalt not forswear thyself, but shalt perform unto the LORD thine oaths: but I say unto you, swear not at all; neither by the heaven, for it is the throne of GOD; nor by the earth, for it is the footstool of HIS feet; nor by Jerusalem, for it is the city of the great KING. Neither shalt thou swear by thy head, for thou canst not make one hair white or black. But let your speech be, Yea, yea; Nay, nay: and whatsoever is more than these is of the evil one. Ye have heard that it was said, An eye for an eye, and a tooth for a tooth: but I say unto you, resist not him that is evil: but whosoever smiteth thee on thy right cheek, turn to him the other also. And if any man would go to law with thee, and take away thy coat, let him have thy cloak also. And whosoever shall compel thee to go one mile, go with him two. Give to him that asketh thee, and from him that would borrow of thee turn not thou away. Ye have heard that it was said, Thou shalt love thy neighbor, and hate thine enemy: but I say unto you, love your enemies, and pray for them that persecute you; that ye may be sons of your FATHER WHO is in heaven: for HE maketh HIS sun to rise on the evil and the good, and sendeth rain on the just and the unjust. For if ye love them that love you, what reward have ye? do not even the publicans the same? And if ye salute your brethren only, what do ye more than others? do not even the Gentiles the same? Ye therefore shall be perfect, as your heavenly FATHER is perfect."

Ω

Righteousness in GOD's view is obedience in action. If I have transgressed against GOD or man, then it is not enough to feel bad, or not obliging restitution because it put me in a bad situation. My deliberate thoughts and actions must be in the comforting knowledge, that because of doing what is right according to HIS WORD, HE is pleased. Where does HE declare, what is right? *The Holy Bible.*

A

Isaiah 45:19, "I (GOD) have not spoken in secret, in a place of the land of darkness; I said not unto the seed of Jacob, Seek ye me in vain: I, JEHOVAH, speak righteousness, I declare things that are right."

Ω

The Holy Bible in its entirety is the written culmination of GOD's will for me to govern my behavior. Understand, the HOLY SPIRIT is the power, WHO educates and empowers me to perform actions or inactions in accordance with GOD's desires for good. A basic principle of righteousness is the implementation of HIS love towards people.

PATIENCE

Chapter 7

When I think of patience, I think of its application in my life, and I tend to forget that this is of GOD's character. The character that GOD desires in me are HIS values. Patience is synonymous with quality, and GOD wants to bring out the best in me, which is HIM. From David's youth, he was patient towards GOD's anointing (placed in a position of authority by GOD) him as king, while Saul became a hateful master.

A

1 Samuel 16:11-13, "And Samuel said unto Jesse, Are here all thy children? And he said, There remaineth yet the youngest, and, behold, he is keeping the sheep. And Samuel said unto Jesse, Send and fetch him; for we will not sit down till he come hither. And he sent, and brought him in. Now he was ruddy, and withal of a beautiful countenance, and goodly to look upon. And JEHOVAH said, Arise, anoint him; for this is he. Then Samuel took the horn of oil, and anointed him in the midst of his brethren: and the SPIRIT of JEHOVAH came mightily upon David from that day forward. So Samuel rose up, and went to Ramah."

1 Samuel 16:20-21, "And Jesse took an ass laden with bread, and a bottle of wine, and a kid, and sent them by David his son unto Saul. And David came to Saul, and stood before him: and he loved him greatly; and he became his armorbearer."

1 Samuel 18:5, "And David went out whithersoever Saul sent him, and behaved himself wisely: and Saul set him over the men of war, and it was good in the sight of all the people, and also in the sight of Saul's servants."

Ω

71

Saul's pride caused him to become hateful, but David is still obedient in implementing Saul's instructions. David tried to please Saul. Later, Saul wanted to keep David close in order to limit his sphere of influence, and hoped David would be slain in combat.

A

1 Samuel 18:6-30, "And it came to pass as they came, when David returned from the slaughter of the Philistine, that the women came out of all the cities of Israel, singing and dancing, to meet king Saul, with timbrels, with joy, and with instruments of music. And the women sang one to another as they played, and said, Saul hath slain his thousands, And David his ten thousands. And Saul was very wroth, and this saying displeased him; and he said, They have ascribed unto David ten thousands, and to me they have ascribed but thousands: and what can he have more but the kingdom? And Saul eyed David from that day and forward. And it came to pass on the morrow, that an evil spirit from GOD came mightily upon Saul, and he prophesied in the midst of the house: and David played with his hand, as he did day by day. And Saul had his spear in his hand; and Saul cast the spear; for he said, I will smite David even to the wall. And David avoided out of his presence twice. And Saul was afraid of David, because JEHOVAH was with him, and was departed from Saul. Therefore Saul removed him from him, and made him his captain over a thousand; and he went out and came in before the people. And David behaved himself wisely in all his ways; and JEHOVAH was with him. And when Saul saw that he behaved himself very wisely, he stood in awe of him. But all Israel and Judah loved David; for he went out and came in before them. And Saul said to David, Behold, my elder daughter Merab, her will I give thee to wife: only be thou valiant for me, and fight JEHOVAH's battles. For Saul said, Let not my hand be upon him, but let the hand of the Philistines be upon him. And David said unto Saul, Who am I, and what is my life, or my father's family in Israel, that I should be son-in-law to the king?

But it came to pass at the time when Merab, Saul's daughter, should have been given to David, that she was given unto Adriel the Meholathite to wife. And Michal, Saul's daughter, loved David: and they told Saul, and the thing pleased him. And Saul said, I will give him her, that she may be a snare to him, and that the hand of the Philistines may be against him. Wherefore Saul said to David, Thou shalt this day be my son-in-law a second time. And Saul commanded his servants, saying, Commune with David secretly, and say, Behold, the king hath delight in thee, and all his servants love thee: now therefore be the king's son-in-law. And Saul's servants spake those words in the ears of David. And David said, Seemeth it to you a light thing to be the king's son-in-law, seeing that I am a poor man, and lightly esteemed? And the servants of Saul told him, saying, On this manner spake David. And Saul said, Thus shall ye say to David, The king desireth not any dowry, but a hundred foreskins of the Philistines, to be avenged of the king's enemies. Now Saul thought to make David fall by the hand of the Philistines. And when his servants told David these words, it pleased David well to be the king's son-in-law. And the days were not expired; and David arose and went, he and his men, and slew of the Philistines two hundred men; and David brought their foreskins, and they gave them in full number to the king, that he might be the king's son-in-law. And Saul gave him Michal his daughter to wife. And Saul saw and knew that JEHOVAH was with David; and Michal, Saul's daughter, loved him. And Saul was yet the more afraid of David; and Saul was David's enemy continually. Then the princes of the Philistines went forth: and it came to pass, as often as they went forth, that David behaved himself more wisely than all the servants of Saul; so that his name was much set by."

Ω

By marrying Michal, Saul's daughter, David became part of the royal family, and King Saul attempted to slay David again. David realized he had to get away from Saul in order to survive. David fled King Saul's presence with the aid of Michal, Samuel, and Ahimelech.

A

1 Samuel 19:9-14, "And an evil spirit from JEHOVAH was upon Saul, as he sat in his house with his spear in his hand; and David was playing with his hand. And Saul sought to smite David even to the wall with the spear; but he slipped away out of Saul's presence, and he smote the spear into the wall: and David fled, and escaped that night. And Saul sent messengers unto David's house, to watch him, and to slay him in the morning: and Michal, David's wife, told him, saying, If thou save not thy life to-night, to-morrow thou wilt be slain. So Michal let David down through the window: and he went, and fled, and escaped. And Michal took the teraphim, and laid it in the bed, and put a pillow of goats' hair at the head thereof, and covered it with the clothes. And when Saul sent messengers to take David, she said, He is sick."

1 Samuel 19:18-24, "Now David fled, and escaped, and came to Samuel to Ramah, and told him all that Saul had done to him. And he and Samuel went and dwelt in Naioth. And it was told Saul, saying, Behold, David is at Naioth in Ramah. And Saul sent messengers to take David: and when they saw the company of the prophets prophesying, and Samuel standing as head over them, the SPIRIT of GOD came upon the messengers of Saul, and they also prophesied. And when it was told Saul, he sent other messengers, and they also prophesied. And Saul sent messengers again the third time, and they also prophesied. Then went he also to Ramah, and came to the great well that is in Secu: and he asked and said, Where are Samuel and David? And one said, Behold, they are at Naioth in Ramah. And he went thither to Naioth in Ramah: and the SPIRIT of GOD came upon him also, and he went on, and prophesied, until he came to Naioth in Ramah. And he also stripped off his clothes, and he also prophesied before Samuel, and lay down naked all that day and all that night. Wherefore they say, Is Saul also among the prophets?"

1 Samuel 21:1-9, "Then came David to Nob to Ahimelech the priest: and Ahimelech came to meet David trembling, and said unto him, Why art thou alone, and no man with thee? And David said unto Ahimelech the priest, The king hath commanded me a business, and hath said unto me, Let no man know anything of the business whereabout I send thee, and what I have commanded thee: and I have appointed the young men to such and such a place. Now therefore what is under thy hand? give me five loaves of bread in my hand, or whatsoever there is present. And the priest answered David, and said, There is no common bread under my hand, but there is holy bread; if only the young men have kept themselves from women. And David answered the priest, and said unto him, Of a truth women have been kept from us about these three days; when I came out, the vessels of the young men were holy, though it was but a common journey; how much more then to-day shall their vessels be holy? So the priest gave him holy bread; for there was no bread there but the showbread, that was taken from before JEHOVAH, to put hot bread in the day when it was taken away. Now a certain man of the servants of Saul was there that day, detained before JEHOVAH; and his name was Doeg the Edomite, the chiefest of the herdsmen that belonged to Saul. And David said unto Ahimelech, And is there not here under thy hand spear or sword? for I have neither brought my sword nor my weapons with me, because the king's business required haste. And the priest said, The sword of Goliath the Philistine, whom thou slewest in the vale of Elah, behold, it is here wrapped in a cloth behind the ephod: if thou wilt take that, take it; for there is no other save that here. And David said, There is none like that; give it me."

Ω

Patience matures by waiting for GOD to open a door instead of me forcing my way. David had an opportunity for vengeance against his master, King Saul, but by sparing Saul, David refused to usurp GOD's judgment. He relinquished vendetta and personal ambition because he recognized that GOD had anointed Saul as king of

Israel. He has a second opportunity to avenge himself, but confirms his resolute spirit in obedience to "The Law."

A

1 Samuel 24:1-22, "And it came to pass, when Saul was returned from following the Philistines, that it was told him, saying, Behold, David is in the wilderness of En-gedi. Then Saul took three thousand chosen men out of all Israel, and went to seek David and his men upon the rocks of the wild goats. And he came to the sheepcotes by the way, where was a cave; and Saul went in to cover his feet. Now David and his men were abiding in the innermost parts of the cave. And the men of David said unto him, Behold, the day of which JEHOVAH said unto thee, Behold, I will deliver thine enemy into thy hand, and thou shalt do to him as it shall seem good unto thee. Then David arose, and cut off the skirt of Saul's robe privily. And it came to pass afterward, that David's heart smote him, because he had cut off Saul's skirt. And he said unto his men, JEHOVAH forbid that I should do this thing unto my lord, JEHOVAH's anointed, to put forth my hand against him, seeing he is JEHOVAH's anointed. So David checked his men with these words, and suffered them not to rise against Saul. And Saul rose up out of the cave, and went on his way. David also arose afterward, and went out of the cave, and cried after Saul, saying, My lord the king. And when Saul looked behind him, David bowed with his face to the earth, and did obeisance. And David said to Saul Wherefore hearkenest thou to men's words, saying, Behold, David seeketh thy hurt? Behold, this day thine eyes have seen how that JEHOVAH had delivered thee to-day into my hand in the cave: and some bade me kill thee; but mine eye spared thee; and I said, I will not put forth my hand against my lord; for he is JEHOVAH's anointed. Moreover, my father, see, yea, see the skirt of thy robe in my hand; for in that I cut off the skirt of thy robe, and killed thee not, know thou and see that there is neither evil nor transgression in my hand, and I have not sinned against thee, though thou huntest after my life to take it. JEHOVAH judge between me and

76

thee, and JEHOVAH avenge me of thee; but my hand shall not be upon thee. As saith the proverb of the ancients, Out of the wicked cometh forth wickedness; but my hand shall not be upon thee. After whom is the king of Israel come out? after whom dost thou pursue? after a dead dog, after a flea. JEHOVAH therefore be judge, and give sentence between me and thee, and see, and plead my cause, and deliver me out of thy hand. And it came to pass, when David had made an end of speaking these words unto Saul, that Saul said, Is this thy voice, my son David? And Saul lifted up his voice, and wept. And he said to David, Thou art more righteous than I; for thou hast rendered unto me good, whereas I have rendered unto thee evil. And thou hast declared this day how that thou hast dealt well with me, forasmuch as when JEHOVAH had delivered me up into thy hand, thou killedst me not. For if a man find his enemy, will he let him go well away? Wherefore JEHOVAH reward thee good for that which thou hast done unto me this day. And now, behold, I know that thou shalt surely be king, and that the kingdom of Israel shall be established in thy hand. Swear now therefore unto me by JEHOVAH, that thou wilt not cut off my seed after me, and that thou wilt not destroy my name out of my father's house. And David sware unto Saul. And Saul went home; but David and his men gat them up unto the stronghold."

1 Samuel 26:1-25, "And the Ziphites came unto Saul to Gibeah, saying, Doth not David hide himself in the hill of Hachilah, which is before the desert? Then Saul arose, and went down to the wilderness of Ziph, having three thousand chosen men of Israel with him, to seek David in the wilderness of Ziph. And Saul encamped in the hill of Hachilah, which is before the desert, by the way. But David abode in the wilderness, and he saw that Saul came after him into the wilderness. David therefore sent out spies, and understood that Saul was come of a certainty. And David arose, and came to the place where Saul had encamped; and David beheld the place where Saul lay, and Abner the son of Ner, the captain of his host: and Saul lay within the place of the wagons, and the people were encamped round about him. Then answered David and said to Ahimelech the Hittite, and to Abishai the son of Zeruiah, brother to Joab, saying, Who will go down with me to Saul to the camp? And Abishai said, I will go down with thee. So David and Abishai came to the people by night: and, behold, Saul lay sleeping within the place of the wagons, with his spear stuck in the ground at his head; and Abner and the people lay round about him. Then said Abishai to David, GOD hath delivered up thine enemy into thy hand this day: now therefore let me smite him, I pray thee, with the spear to the earth at one stroke, and I will not smite him the second time. And David said to Abishai, Destroy him not; for who can put forth his hand against JEHOVAH's anointed, and be guiltless? And David said, As JEHOVAH liveth, JEHOVAH will smite him; or his day shall come to die; or he shall go down into battle and perish. JEHOVAH forbid that I should put forth my hand against JEHOVAH's anointed: but now take, I pray thee, the spear that is at his head, and the cruse of water, and let us go. So David took the spear and the cruse of water from Saul's head; and they gat them away: and no man saw it, nor knew it, neither did any awake; for they were all asleep, because a deep sleep from JEHOVAH was fallen upon them. Then David went over to the other side, and stood on the top of the mountain afar off; a great space being between them; and David cried to the people, and to Abner the son of Ner, saying, Answerest thou not, Abner? Then Abner answered and said, Who art thou that criest to the king? And David said to Abner, Art not thou a valiant man? and who is like to thee in Israel? wherefore then hast thou not kept watch over thy lord the king? for there came one of the people in to destroy the king thy lord. This thing is not good that thou hast done. As JEHOVAH liveth, ye are worthy to die, because ye have not kept watch over your lord, JEHOVAH's anointed. And now see where the king's spear is, and the cruse of water that was at his head. And Saul knew David's voice, and said, Is this thy voice, my son David? And David said, It is my voice, my lord, O king. And he said, Wherefore doth my lord pursue after his servant? for what have I done? or what evil is in my hand? Now therefore, I pray thee, let my lord the king hear the words of his servant. If it be JEHOVAH that hath stirred thee up against me, let HIM accept an offering: but if it be the children of men, cursed be they before JEHOVAH: for they have driven me out this day that I should not

78

cleave unto the inheritance of JEHOVAH, saying, Go, serve other gods. Now therefore, let not my blood fall to the earth away from the presence of JEHOVAH: for the king of Israel is come out to seek a flea, as when one doth hunt a partridge in the mountains. Then said Saul, I have sinned: return, my son David; for I will no more do thee harm, because my life was precious in thine eyes this day: behold, I have played the fool, and have erred exceedingly. And David answered and said, Behold the spear, O king! let then one of the young men come over and fetch it. And JEHOVAH will render to every man his righteousness and his faithfulness; forasmuch as JEHOVAH delivered thee into my hand to-day, and I would not put forth my hand against JEHOVAH's anointed. And, behold, as thy life was much set by this day in mine eyes, so let my life be much set by in the eyes of JEHOVAH, and let HIM deliver me out of all tribulation. Then Saul said to David, Blessed be thou, my son David: thou shalt both do mightily, and shalt surely prevail. So David went his way, and Saul returned to his place."

Ω

After David endured tribulations, King Saul dies in battle, and David became king. Through David's patience the men of Judah anoint David as their king. GOD confirms my place in his kingdom by revelation and people.

A

1 Samuel 31:1-6, "Now the Philistines fought against Israel: and the men of Israel fled from before the Philistines, and fell down slain in mount Gilboa. And the Philistines followed hard upon Saul and upon his sons; and the Philistines slew Jonathan, and Abinadab, and Malchi-shua, the sons of Saul. And the battle went sore against Saul, and the archers overtook him; and he was greatly distressed by reason of the archers. Then said Saul to his armorbearer, Draw thy sword, and thrust me through therewith, lest these uncircumcised come and thrust me through, and abuse me. But his armorbearer would not; for he was sore afraid. Therefore Saul took his sword, and fell upon it. And when his armorbearer saw that Saul was dead, he likewise fell upon his sword, and died with him. So Saul died, and his three sons, and his armorbearer, and all his men, that same day together."

2 Samuel 2:1-7, "And it came to pass after this, that David inquired of JEHOVAH, saying, Shall I go up into any of the cities of Judah? And JEHOVAH said unto him, Go up. And David said, Whither shall I go up? And he said, Unto Hebron. So David went up thither, and his two wives also, Ahinoam the Jezreelitess, and Abigail the wife of Nabal the Carmelite. And his men that were with him did David bring up, every man with his household: and they dwelt in the cities of Hebron. And the men of Judah came, and there they anointed David king over the house of Judah. And David sent messengers unto the men of Jabesh-gilead, and said unto them, Blessed be ye of JEHOVAH, that ye have showed this kindness unto your lord, even unto Saul, and have buried him. And now JEHOVAH show lovingkindness and truth unto you: and I also will requite you this kindness, because ye have done this thing. Now therefore let your hands be strong, and be ye valiant; for Saul your lord is dead, and also the house of Judah have anointed me king over them."

Ω

GOD spoke to Abram when he was seventy-five years old, instructing him to leave his father's house. GOD initiates the process of Abram's faith, and these next scriptures identify his shortcomings, but he eventually developed resolute faith settling in the plain of Moreh exactly where he began. That is where he found GOD.

A

Genesis 12:1-4, "Now JEHOVAH said unto Abram, Get thee out of thy country, and from thy kindred, and from thy father's house, unto the land that I will show thee: and I will make of thee a great nation, and I will bless thee, and make thy name great; and be thou a blessing; and I will bless them that bless thee, and him that curseth thee will I curse: and in thee shall all the families of the earth be blessed. So Abram went, as JEHOVAH had spoken unto him; and Lot went with him: and Abram was seventy and five years old when he departed out of Haran."

Genesis 12:6-7, "And Abram passed through the land unto the place of Shechem, unto the oak of Moreh. And the Canaanite was then in the land. And JEHOVAH appeared unto Abram, and said, Unto thy seed will I give this land: and there builded he an altar unto JEHOVAH, WHO appeared unto him. And he removed from thence unto the mountain on the east of Beth-el, and pitched his tent, having Beth-el on the west, and Ai on the east: and there he builded an altar unto JEHOVAH, and called upon the name of JEHOVAH."

Genesis 12:10-13:17, "And there was a famine in the land: and Abram went down into Egypt to sojourn there; for the famine was sore in the land. And it came to pass, when he was come near to enter into Egypt, that he said unto Sarai his wife, Behold now, I know that thou art a fair woman to look upon: and it will come to pass, when the Egyptians shall see thee, that they will say, This is his wife: and they will kill me, but they will save thee alive. Say, I pray thee, thou art my sister; that it may be well with me for thy sake, and that my soul may live because of thee. And it came to pass, that, when Abram was come into Egypt, the Egyptians beheld the woman that she was very fair. And the princes of Pharaoh saw her, and praised her to Pharaoh: and the woman was taken into Pharaoh's house. And he dealt well with Abram for her sake: and he had sheep, and oxen, and he-asses, and men-servants, and maid-servants, and she-asses, and camels. And JEHOVAH plagued Pharaoh and his house with great plagues because of Sarai, Abram's wife. And Pharaoh called Abram, and said, What is this that thou hast done unto me? why didst thou not tell me that she was thy wife? why saidst thou, She is my sister, so that I took her to be my wife? now therefore behold thy wife, take her, and go thy way. And Pharaoh gave men charge concerning him: and they brought him on the way, and his wife, and all that he had. And Abram went up out of Egypt, he, and his wife, and all that he had, and Lot with him, into the South. And Abram was very rich in cattle, in silver, and in gold. And he went on his journeys from the South even to Beth-el, unto the place where his tent had been at the beginning, between Beth-el and Ai, unto the place of the altar, which he had made there at the first: and there Abram called on the name of JEHOVAH. And Lot also, who went with Abram, had flocks, and herds, and tents. And the land was not able to bear them, that they might dwell together: for their substance was great, so that they could not dwell together. And there was a strife between the herdsmen of Abram's cattle and the herdsmen of Lot's cattle: and the Canaanite and the Perizzite dwelt then in the land. And Abram said unto Lot, Let there be no strife, I pray thee, between me and thee, and between my herdsmen and thy herdsmen; for we are brethren. Is not the whole land before thee? separate thyself, I pray thee, from me. If thou wilt take the left hand, then I will go to the right. Or if thou take the right hand, then I will go to the left. And Lot lifted up his eyes, and beheld all the Plain of the Jordan, that it was well watered every where, before JEHOVAH destroyed Sodom and Gomorrah, like the garden of JEHOVAH, like the land of Egypt, as thou goest unto Zoar. So Lot chose him all the Plain of the Jordan; and Lot journeyed east: and they separated themselves the one from the other. Abram dwelt in the land of Canaan, and Lot dwelt in the cities of the Plain, and moved his tent as far as Sodom. Now the men of Sodom were wicked and sinners against JEHOVAH exceedingly. And JEHOVAH said unto Abram, after that Lot was separated from him, Lift up now thine eyes, and look from the place where thou art, northward and southward and eastward and westward: for all the land which thou seest, to thee will I give it, and to thy seed for ever. And I will make thy seed as the dust of the earth: so that if a man can number the dust of the earth, then may thy seed also be numbered. Arise, walk through the land in the length of it and in the breadth of it; for unto thee will I give it."

Ω

In scripture, the word "wait" is an action word for "patient." GOD is keenly aware of what HE has for me, I do not have to rush before my time runs out. HE wants me to be still, wait for HIM to set the stage because then HE will perform in ways I did not imagine to HIS glory. The very multitude of scriptures that confirm this are plentiful, but here are a few.

A

Psalms 27:13-14, "I had fainted, unless I had believed to see the goodness of JEHOVAH In the land of the living. Wait for JEHOVAH: Be strong, and let thy heart take courage; Yea, wait thou for JEHOVAH."

Psalms 37:7-9, "Rest in JEHOVAH, and wait patiently for HIM: Fret not thyself because of him who prospereth in his way, Because of the man who bringeth wicked devices to pass. Cease from anger, and forsake wrath: Fret not thyself, it tendeth only to evil-doing. For evildoers shall be cut off; But those that wait for JEHOVAH, they shall inherit the land."

Galatians 5:5, "For we through the SPIRIT by faith wait for the hope of righteousness."

Ω

Scripture also refers to GOD's patience as long-suffering; whenever, HE is waiting for my repentance and obedience. GOD wants me to succeed, and that takes obedience on my part. HE is long-suffering toward me to understand, that HE also wants me to believe HIS purpose for me is to succeed.

A

Exodus 34:4-7, "And he (Moses) hewed two tables of stone like unto the first; and Moses rose up early in the morning, and went up unto mount Sinai, as JEHOVAH had commanded him, and took in his hand two tables of stone. And JEHOVAH descended in the cloud, and stood with him there, and proclaimed the name of JEHOVAH. And JEHOVAH passed by before him, and proclaimed, JEHOVAH, JEHOVAH, a GOD merciful and gracious, slow to anger, and abundant in lovingkindness and truth, keeping lovingkindness for thousands, forgiving iniquity and transgression and sin; and that will by no means clear the guilty, visiting the iniquity of the fathers upon the children, and upon the children's children, upon the third and upon the fourth generation."

Psalms 86:11-17, "Teach me thy way, O JEHOVAH; I will walk in thy truth: Unite my heart to fear THY name. I will praise THEE, O LORD my GOD, with my whole heart; And I will glorify THY name for evermore. For great is THY lovingkindness toward me; And THOU hast delivered my soul from the lowest Sheol. O GOD, the proud are risen up against me, And a company of violent men have sought after my soul, And have not set THEE before them. But THOU, O LORD, art a GOD merciful and gracious, Slow to anger, and abundant in lovingkindness and truth. Oh turn unto me, and have mercy upon me; Give THY strength unto THY servant, And save the son of THY handmaid. Show me a token for good, That they who hate me may see it, and be put to shame, Because THOU, JEHOVAH, hast helped me, and comforted me."

2 Peter 3:9, "The LORD is not slack concerning HIS promise, as some count slackness; but is longsuffering to you-ward, not wishing that any should perish, but that all should come to repentance."

Ω

GOD is patient with the children of Israel despite unbelief and ungratefulness of GOD's provision. HE addresses HIS long-suffering tolerance of their actions, and how that generation grieved HIM as HE patiently waited for their unrepentant hearts to evolve. It is naive to think living a nomadic lifestyle, and eating the same food for years is effortless. I find myself wondering if I would be groaning and complaining like them.

A

Psalms 95:8-11, "Harden not your heart, as at Meribah, As in the day of Massah in the wilderness; When your fathers tempted ME, Proved ME, and saw MY work. Forty years long was I grieved with that generation, And said, It is a people that do err in their heart, And they have not known MY ways: Wherefore I sware in MY wrath, That they should not enter into MY rest."

Ω

Try eating the same food every day for a month. I would hope and depend on GOD to do it without complaining, and then I may have an inclination of how they felt. It concerns me because the heritage of my forefathers' behavior is biologically graphed in me all the way back to Adam, and JESUS acknowledges it. I am in no better disposition than them, and I recognize that **only** through HIS SPIRIT I am able to accomplish HIS will.

A

Matthew 23:29-32, (JESUS speaking) "Woe unto you, scribes and Pharisees, hypocrites! for ye build the sepulchres of the prophets, and garnish the tombs of the righteous, and say, If we had been in the days of our fathers, we should not have been partakers with them in the blood of the prophets. Wherefore ye witness to yourselves, that ye are sons of them that slew the prophets. Fill ye up then the measure of your fathers."

Luke 6:17-26, "and HE (JESUS) came down with them (the twelve disciples), and stood on a level place, and a great multitude of HIS disciples, and a great number of the people from all Judaea and Jerusalem, and the sea coast of Tyre and Sidon, who came to hear HIM, and to be healed of their diseases; and they that were troubled with unclean spirits were healed. And all the multitude sought to touch HIM; for power came forth from HIM, and healed them all. And HE lifted up HIS eyes on HIS disciples, and said, Blessed are ye poor: for yours is the kingdom of GOD. Blessed are ye that hunger now: for ye shall be filled. Blessed are ye that weep now: for ye shall laugh. Blessed are ye, when men shall hate you, and when they shall separate you from their company, and reproach you, and cast out your name as evil, for the SON of man's sake. Rejoice in that day, and leap for joy: for behold, your reward is great in heaven; for in the same manner did their fathers unto the prophets. But woe unto you that are rich! for ye have received your consolation. Woe unto you, ye that are full now! for ye shall hunger. Woe unto you, ye that laugh now! for ye shall mourn and weep. Woe unto you, when all men shall speak well of you! for in the same manner did their fathers to the false prophets."

Ω

GOD searches for obedience, so that HE will reward me. I am included in one of the people he is waiting to bless. GOD patiently waited forty years to raise an obedient generation, so they would reap the covenant benefits offered to their fathers.

A

Numbers 14:26-34, "And JEHOVAH spake unto Moses and unto Aaron, saying, How long shall I bear with this evil congregation, that murmur against ME? I have heard the murmurings of the children of Israel, which they murmur against ME. Say unto them, As I live, saith JEHOVAH, surely as ye have spoken in MINE ears, so will I do to you: your dead bodies shall fall in this wilderness; and all that were numbered of you, according to your whole number, from twenty years old and upward, that have murmured against ME, surely ye shall not come into the land, concerning which I sware that I would make you dwell therein, save Caleb the son of Jephunneh, and Joshua the son of Nun. But your little ones, that ye said should be a prey, them will I bring in, and they shall know the land which ye have rejected. But as for you, your dead bodies shall fall in this wilderness. And your children shall be wanderers in the wilderness forty years, and shall bear your whoredoms, until your dead bodies be consumed in the wilderness. After the number of the days in which ye spied out the land, even forty days, for every day a year, shall ye bear your iniquities, even forty years, and ye shall know MY alienation."

Deuteronomy 1:34-39, "And JEHOVAH heard the voice of your words, and was wroth, and sware, saying, Surely there shall not one of these men of this evil generation see the good land, which I sware to give unto your fathers, save Caleb the son of Jephunneh: he shall see it; and to him will I give the land that he hath trodden upon, and to his children, because he hath wholly followed JEHOVAH. Also JEHOVAH was angry with me (Moses) for your sakes, saying, Thou also shalt not go in thither: Joshua the son of Nun, who standeth before thee, he shall go in thither: encourage thou him; for he shall cause Israel to inherit it. Moreover your little ones, that ye said should be a prey, and your children, that this day have no knowledge of good or evil, they shall go in thither, and unto them will I give it, and they shall possess it."

Ω

It is easier for me to comprehend that GOD is being patient with the issues of others, rather than thinking HE is being patient with my issues. In other words, it is easier to notice GOD's mercy on others, than to identify HIS mercy on me. Like any good refiner, HE has to patiently mold me by repeating the process of reheating. Patience produces consistency, and consistency produces reward. HE is also patient to grace me with time in order to repent, like HIS patience with Jezebel.

A

1 Kings 16:31-33, "And it came to pass, as if it had been a light thing for him (King Ahab) to walk in the sins of Jeroboam the son of Nebat, that he took to wife Jezebel the daughter of Ethbaal king of the Sidonians, and went and served Baal, and worshipped him. And he reared up an altar for Baal in the house of Baal, which he had built in Samaria. And Ahab made the Asherah; and Ahab did yet more to provoke JEHOVAH, the GOD of Israel, to anger than all the kings of Israel that were before him."

1 Kings 18:3-4, "And Ahab called Obadiah, who was over the household. (Now Obadiah feared JEHOVAH greatly: for it was so, when Jezebel cut off the prophets of JEHOVAH, that Obadiah took a hundred prophets, and hid them by fifty in a cave, and fed them with bread and water.)"

1 Kings 19:1-2, "And Ahab told Jezebel all that Elijah had done, and withal how he had slain all the prophets with the sword. Then Jezebel send a messenger unto Elijah, saying, So let the gods do to me, and more also, if I make not thy life as the life of one of them by tomorrow about this time."

1 Kings 21:1-16, "And it came to pass after these things, that Naboth the Jezreelite had a vineyard, which was in Jezreel, hard by the palace of Ahab king of Samaria. And Ahab spake unto Naboth, saying, Give me thy vineyard, that I may have it for a garden of herbs, because it is near unto my house; and I will give thee for it a better vineyard than it: or, if it seem good to thee, I will give thee the worth of it in money. And Naboth said to Ahab, JEHOVAH forbid it me, that I should give the inheritance of my fathers unto thee. And Ahab came into his house heavy and displeased because of the word which Naboth the Jezreelite had spoken to him; for he had said, I will not give thee the inheritance of my fathers. And he laid him down upon his bed, and turned away his face, and would eat no bread. But Jezebel his wife came to him, and said unto him, Why is thy spirit so sad, that thou eatest no bread? And he said unto her, Because I spake unto Naboth the Jezreelite, and said unto him, Give me thy vineyard for money; or else, if it please thee, I will give thee another vineyard for it: and he answered, I will not give thee my vineyard. And Jezebel his wife said unto him, Dost thou now govern the kingdom of Israel? arise, and eat bread, and let thy heart be merry: I will give thee the vineyard of Naboth the Jezreelite. So she wrote letters in Ahab's name, and sealed them with his seal, and sent the letters unto the elders and to the nobles that were in his city, and that dwelt with Naboth. And she wrote in the letters, saying, Proclaim a fast, and set Naboth on high among the people: and set two men, base fellows, before him, and let them bear witness against him, saying, Thou didst curse GOD and the king. And then carry him out, and stone him to death. And the men of his city, even the elders and the nobles who dwelt in his city, did as Jezebel had sent unto them, according as it was written in the letters which she had sent unto them. They proclaimed a fast, and set Naboth on high among the people. And the two men, the base fellows, came in and sat before him: and the base fellows bare witness against him, even against Naboth, in the presence of the people, saying, Naboth did curse GOD and the king. Then they carried him forth out of the city, and stoned him to death with stones. Then they sent to Jezebel, saying, Naboth is stoned, and is dead. And it came to pass, when Jezebel heard that Naboth was stoned, and was dead, that Jezebel said to Ahab, Arise, take possession of the vineyard of Naboth the Jezreelite, which he refused to give thee for money; for Naboth is not alive, but dead. And it came to pass, when Ahab heard that Naboth was dead, that Ahab rose up to go down to the vineyard of Naboth the Jezreelite, to take possession of it."

Ezekiel 33:10-11, "And thou, son of man, say unto the house of Israel: Thus ye speak, saying, Our transgressions and our sins are upon us, and we pine away in them; how then can we live? Say unto them, As I live, saith the LORD JEHOVAH, I have no pleasure in the death of the wicked; but that the wicked turn from his way and live: turn ye, turn ye from your evil ways; for why will ye die, O house of Israel?"

Revelation 2:20-21, (JESUS speaking) "But I have this against thee, that thou sufferest the woman Jezebel, who calleth herself a prophetess; and she teacheth and seduceth my servants to commit fornication, and to eat things sacrificed to idols. **And I gave her time that she should repent**; and she willeth not to repent of her fornication."

Ω

GOD knows sin is present in my heart, but HE is allowing me to yield to HIM, and overcome it. HE allows the defiant to coexist in order to make room for repentance or justice. GOD's patience provides room for judgment, and judgment is potentially favorable or unfavorable, but JESUS' life encourages my confidence by HIS investment in my life.

FAITHFULNESS

Chapter 9

Being faithful involves relationships, whether to GOD, myself, or others. Faithfulness is the resolution to responsibility, so in scriptural terms it is fulfillment of my debt, trespass, or obligation. GOD is absolutely adamant about performing HIS WORD, and is faithful because HE yields to that precedent. GOD swears by HIS own being because HE has found HIMSELF to be faithful in every instance. If HE swears by anyone or anything else, then HIS WORD would be open to doubt.

A

Genesis 22:15-18, "And the angel of JEHOVAH called unto Abraham a second time out of heaven, and said, By MYSELF have I sworn, saith JEHOVAH, because thou hast done this thing, and hast not withheld thy son, thine only son, that in blessing I will bless thee, and in multiplying I will multiply thy SEED as the stars of the heavens, and as the sand which is upon the seashore. And thy SEED shall possess the gate of his enemies. And in thy SEED shall all the nations of the earth be blessed. Because thou hast obeyed MY voice."

Ω

Jonathan, King Saul's son, understood how to be faithful regardless of the cost. He was a friend of David, who realize GOD's favor towards David. Jonathan's protection of David guaranteed he would never be king, and JESUS affirms that precept as a prerequisite for salvation.

A

1 Samuel 20:1-42, "And David fled from Naioth in Ramah, and came and said before Jonathan, What have I done? what is mine iniquity?

91

and what is my sin before thy father, that he seeketh my life? And he said unto him, Far from it; thou shalt not die: behold, my father doeth nothing either great or small, but that he discloseth it unto me; and why should my father hide this thing from me? it is not so. And David sware moreover, and said, Thy father knoweth well that I have found favor in thine eyes; and he saith, Let not Jonathan know this, lest he be grieved: but truly as JEHOVAH liveth, and as thy soul liveth, there is but a step between me and death. Then said Jonathan unto David, Whatsoever thy soul desireth, I will even do it for thee. And David said unto Jonathan, Behold, to-morrow is the new moon, and I should not fail to sit with the king at meat: but let me go, that I may hide myself in the field unto the third day at even. If thy father miss me at all, then say, David earnestly asked leave of me that he might run to Beth-lehem his city; for it is the yearly sacrifice there for all the family. If he say thus, It is well; thy servant shall have peace: but if he be wroth, then know that evil is determined by him. Therefore deal kindly with thy servant; for thou hast brought thy servant into a covenant of JEHOVAH with thee: but if there be in me iniquity, slay me thyself; for why shouldest thou bring me to thy father? And Jonathan said, Far be it from thee; for if I should at all know that evil were determined by my father to come upon thee, then would not I tell it thee? Then said David to Jonathan, Who shall tell me if perchance thy father answer thee roughly? And Jonathan said unto David, Come, and let us go out into the field. And they went out both of them into the field. And Jonathan said unto David, JEHOVAH, the GOD of Israel, be witness: when I have sounded my father about this time to-morrow, or the third day, behold, if there be good toward David, shall I not then send unto thee, and disclose it unto thee? JEHOVAH do so to Jonathan, and more also, should it please my father to do thee evil, if I disclose it not unto thee, and send thee away, that thou mayest go in peace: and JEHOVAH be with thee, as HE hath been with my father. And thou shalt not only while yet I live show me the lovingkindness of JEHOVAH, that I die not; but also thou shalt not cut off thy kindness from my house for ever; no, not when JEHOVAH hath cut off the enemies of David every one from the face of the earth. So Jonathan made a covenant with the house of David, saying, And

JEHOVAH will require it at the hand of David's enemies. And Jonathan caused David to swear again, for the love that he had to him; for he loved him as he loved his own soul. Then Jonathan said unto him, To-morrow is the new moon: and thou wilt be missed, because thy seat will be empty. And when thou hast stayed three days, thou shalt go down quickly, and come to the place where thou didst hide thyself when the business was in hand, and shalt remain by the stone Ezel. And I will shoot three arrows on the side thereof, as though I shot at a mark. And, behold, I will send the lad, saying, Go, find the arrows. If I say unto the lad, Behold, the arrows are on this side of thee; take them, and come; for there is peace to thee and no hurt, as JEHOVAH liveth. But if I say thus unto the boy, Behold, the arrows are beyond thee; go thy way; for JEHOVAH hath sent thee away. And as touching the matter which thou and I have spoken of, behold, JEHOVAH is between thee and me for ever. So David hid himself in the field: and when the new moon was come, the king sat him down to eat food. And the king sat upon his seat, as at other times, even upon the seat by the wall; and Jonathan stood up, and Abner sat by Saul's side: but David's place was empty. Nevertheless Saul spake not anything that day: for he thought, Something hath befallen him, he is not clean; surely he is not clean. And it came to pass on the morrow after the new moon, which was the second day, that David's place was empty: and Saul said unto Jonathan his son, Wherefore cometh not the son of Jesse to meat, neither yesterday, nor to-day? And Jonathan answered Saul, David earnestly asked leave of me to go to Beth-lehem: and he said, Let me go, I pray thee; for our family hath a sacrifice in the city; and my brother, he hath commanded me to be there: and now, if I have found favor in thine eyes, let me get away, I pray thee, and see my brethren. Therefore he is not come unto the king's table. Then Saul's anger was kindled against Jonathan, and he said unto him, Thou son of a perverse rebellious woman, do not I know that thou hast chosen the son of Jesse to thine own shame, and unto the shame of thy mother's nakedness? **For as long as the son of Jesse liveth upon the ground, thou shalt not be established, nor thy kingdom**. Wherefore now send and fetch him unto me, for he shall surely die. And Jonathan answered Saul his father, and said unto him,

Wherefore should he be put to death? what hath he done? And Saul cast his spear at him to smite him; whereby Jonathan knew that is was determined of his father to put David to death. So Jonathan arose from the table in fierce anger, and did eat no food the second day of the month; for he was grieved for David, because his father had done him shame. And it came to pass in the morning, that Jonathan went out into the field at the time appointed with David, and a little lad with him. And he said unto his lad, Run, find now the arrows which I shoot. And as the lad ran, he shot an arrow beyond him. And when the lad was come to the place of the arrow which Jonathan had shot, Jonathan cried after the lad, and said, Is not the arrow beyond thee? And Jonathan cried after the lad, Make speed, haste, stay not. And Jonathan's lad gathered up the arrows, and came to his master. But the lad knew not anything: only Jonathan and David knew the matter. And Jonathan gave his weapons unto his lad, and said unto him, Go, carry them to the city. And as soon as the lad was gone, David arose out of a place toward the South, and fell on his face to the ground, and bowed himself three times: and they kissed one another, and wept one with another, until David exceeded. And Jonathan said to David, Go in peace, forasmuch as we have sworn both of us in the name of JEHOVAH, saying, JEHOVAH shall be between me and thee, and between my seed and thy seed, for ever. And he arose and departed: and Jonathan went into the city."

Matthew 16:24-26, "Then said JESUS unto HIS disciples, If any man would come after ME, let him deny himself, and take up his cross, and follow ME. For whosoever would save his life shall lose it: and whosoever shall lose his life for MY sake shall find it. For what shall a man be profited, if he shall gain the whole world, and forfeit his life? or what shall a man give in exchange for his life?"

Ω

Faithful bible heroes had faithful dispositions, but they all had an understanding of attributes that GOD values in order to grow spiritually. They had to submit their thought process to GOD's process of faith. GOD subjects me to trials in order to reward my faithfulness to HIS values. The secular system rewards people with ambition, so a person forces themselves by will or by power to accomplish a desired resolution. Even the institutions like the Church are vulnerable to the gravity of wealth, power, significance, and corruption.

A

Hebrews 11:1-38, "Now faith is assurance of things hoped for, a conviction of things not seen. For therein the elders had witness borne to them. By faith we understand that the worlds have been framed by the WORD of GOD, so that what is seen hath not been made out of things which appear. By faith Abel offered unto GOD a more excellent sacrifice than Cain, through which he had witness borne to him that he was righteous, GOD bearing witness in respect of his gifts: and through it he being dead yet speaketh. By faith Enoch was translated that he should not see death; and he was not found, because GOD translated him: for he hath had witness borne to him that before his translation he had been well-pleasing unto GOD: And without faith it is impossible to be well-pleasing unto HIM; for he that cometh to GOD must believe that HE is, and by faith Noah, being warned of GOD concerning things not seen as yet, moved with GODly fear, prepared an ark to the saving of his house; through which he condemned the world, and became heir of the righteousness which is according to faith. By faith Abraham, when he was called, obeyed to go out unto a place which he was to receive for an inheritance; and he went out, not knowing whither he went. By faith he became a sojourner in the land of promise, as in a land not his own, dwelling in tents, with Isaac and Jacob, the heirs with him of the same promise: for he looked for the city which hath the foundations, whose builder and maker is GOD. By faith even Sarah herself received power to conceive seed when she was past age, since she counted HIM faithful WHO had promised: wherefore also there sprang of one, and him as good as dead, so many as the stars of heaven in multitude, and as the sand, which is by the sea-shore, innumerable. These all died in faith, not having received the promises, but having seen them and greeted them from afar, and having confessed that they were strangers and pilgrims on the earth. For they that say such things make it manifest that they are seeking after a country of their own. And if indeed they had been mindful of that country from which they went out, they would have had opportunity to return. But now they desire a better country, that is, a heavenly: wherefore GOD is not ashamed of them, to be called their GOD; for HE hath prepared for them a city. By faith Abraham, being tried, offered up Isaac: yea, he that had gladly received the promises was offering up his only begotten even he to whom it was said, In Isaac shall thy SEED be called: accounting that GOD is able to raise up, even from the dead; from whence he did also in a figure receive him back. By faith Isaac blessed Jacob and Esau, even concerning things to come. By faith Jacob, when he was dying, blessed each of the sons of Joseph; and worshipped, leaning upon the top of his staff. By faith Joseph, when his end was nigh, made mention of the departure of the children of Israel; and gave commandment concerning his bones. By faith Moses, when he was born, was hid three months by his parents, because they saw he was a goodly child; and they were not afraid of the king's commandment. By faith Moses, when he was grown up, refused to be called the son of Pharaoh's daughter; choosing rather to share ill treatment with the people of GOD, than to enjoy the pleasures of sin for a season; accounting the reproach of CHRIST greater riches than the treasures of Egypt: for he looked unto the recompense of reward. By faith he forsook Egypt, not fearing the wrath of the king: for he endured, as seeing HIM who is invisible. By faith he kept the passover, and the sprinkling of the blood, that the destroyer of the firstborn should not touch them. By faith they passed through the Red sea as by dry land: which the Egyptians assaying to do were swallowed up. By faith the walls of Jericho fell down, after they had been compassed about for seven days. By faith Rahab the harlot perished not with them that were disobedient, having received the spies with peace. And what shall I more say? for the time will fail me if I tell of Gideon, Barak, Samson, Jephthah; of David and Samuel and the prophets: who through faith subdued kingdoms, wrought righteousness, obtained promises, stopped the mouths of lions, quenched the power of fire, escaped the edge of the sword, from weakness were made strong, waxed mighty in war, turned to flight armies of aliens. Women received their dead by a resurrection: and others were tortured, not accepting their deliverance; that they might obtain a better resurrection: and others had trial of mockings and scourgings, yea, moreover of bonds and imprisonment: they were stoned, they were sawn asunder, they were tempted, they were slain with the sword: they went about in sheepskins, in goatskins; being destitute, afflicted, ill-treated (of whom the world was not worthy), wandering in deserts and mountains and caves, and the holes of the earth."

Matthew 11:12, (JESUS speaking) "And from the days of John the Baptist until now the kingdom of heaven suffereth violence, and men of violence take it by force."

Ω

GOD allows me to have and achieve goals, but HE does not want me to impose my goals on others without considering their rights and goals. *The Holy Bible* contains scriptures concerning warfare, and reveals anyone without the desire to fight does not have to engage in combat. If GOD did not require all the Hebrews to go to fight before entering into "The Promise Land," and this was a critical moment in their history potentially facing annihilation, then how does HE react to me forcing my will on others?

In part, being faithful is comprising my will to the will of others without violating anyone's rights, and perhaps foregoing my own rights. GOD is patiently progressing me into faithfulness. GOD desires me to be faithful to HIS commands and principles, because HE knows I need HIM, and HE cannot violate HIS WORD, therefore if I am disobedient or unfaithful, then I hinder HIS blessing.

A

Deuteronomy 20:1-8, "When thou goest forth to battle against thine enemies, and seest horses, and chariots, and a people more than thou, thou shalt not be afraid of them; for JEHOVAH thy GOD is with thee, WHO brought thee up out of the land of Egypt. And it shall be, when ye draw nigh unto the battle, that the priest shall approach and speak unto the people, and shall say unto them, Hear, O Israel, ye draw nigh this day unto battle against your enemies: let not your heart faint; fear not, nor tremble, neither be ye affrighted at them; for JEHOVAH your GOD is HE that goeth with you, to fight for you against your enemies, to save you. And the officers shall speak unto the people, saying, What man is there that hath built a new house, and hath not dedicated it? let him go and return to his house, lest he die in the battle, and another man dedicate it. And what man is there that hath planted a vineyard, and hath not used the fruit thereof? let him go and return unto his house, lest he die in the battle, and another man use the fruit thereof. And what man is there that hath betrothed a wife, and hath not taken her? let him go and return unto his house, lest he die in the battle, and another man take her. And the officers shall speak further unto the people, and they shall say, What man is there that is fearful and faint-hearted? let him go and return unto his house, lest his brethren's heart melt as his heart."

Ω

Faithfulness to any person or institution is flawed by self-preservation, so that thing eventually destroys me to protect itself, and because people or institutions are flawed, they skew their presentation to present a pristine image. The Church is an institution established by JESUS, but within the Church are organizations and denominations run by people. People have agendas, intentions, and motivations that are hidden from me or obscure, and only GOD knows the thoughts of their hearts.

A

Psalms 7:8-9, "JEHOVAH ministereth judgment to the peoples: Judge me, O JEHOVAH, according to my righteousness, and to mine integrity that is in me. O let the wickedness of the wicked come to an end, but establish THOU the righteous: For the righteous GOD trieth the minds and hearts."

Luke 5:21-26, "And the scribes and the Pharisees began to reason, saying, WHO is this that speaketh blasphemies? WHO can forgive sins, but GOD alone? But JESUS perceiving their reasonings, answered and said unto them, Why reason ye in your hearts? Which is easier, to say, Thy sins are forgiven thee; or to say, Arise and walk? But that ye may know that the SON of man hath authority on earth to forgive sins (HE said unto him that was palsied), I say unto thee, Arise, and take up thy couch, and go unto thy house. And immediately he rose up before them, and took up that whereon he lay, and departed to his house, glorifying GOD. And amazement took hold on all, and they glorified GOD; and they were filled with fear, saying, We have seen strange things to-day."

Luke 6:6-11, "And it came to pass on another sabbath, that HE (JESUS) entered into the synagogue and taught: and there was a man there, and his right hand was withered. And the scribes and the Pharisees watched HIM, whether HE would heal on the sabbath; that they might find how to accuse HIM. But HE knew their thoughts; and HE said to the man that had his hand withered, Rise up, and stand forth in the midst. And he arose and stood forth. And JESUS said unto them, I ask you, Is it lawful on the sabbath to do good, or to do harm? to save a life, or to destroy it? And HE looked round about on them all, and said unto him, Stretch forth thy hand. And he did so: and his hand was restored. But they were filled with madness; and communed one with another what they might do to JESUS."

Ω

GOD wants me to submit to authority, but not to put my hope and trust in worldly methods. HIS desire is that my faith is in HIM alone. GOD will place people in authority over me to prove my faithfulness to HIM. The tragic story of Uriah, one of David's mighty men, misplaced his faith in David, a man after GOD's own heart.

A

1 Samuel 13:13-14, "And Samuel said to Saul, Thou hast done foolishly; thou hast not kept the commandment of JEHOVAH thy GOD, which he commanded thee: for now would JEHOVAH have established thy kingdom upon Israel for ever. But now thy kingdom shall not continue: JEHOVAH hath sought him a man after HIS own heart, and JEHOVAH hath appointed him to be prince over HIS people, because thou hast not kept that which JEHOVAH commanded thee."

2 Samuel 11:2-24, "And it came to pass at eventide, that David arose from off his bed, and walked upon the roof of the king's house: and from the roof he saw a woman bathing; and the woman was very beautiful to look upon. And David send and inquired after the woman. And one said, Is not this Bath-sheba, the daughter of Eliam, the wife of Uriah the Hittite? And David sent messengers, and took her; and she came in unto him, and he lay with her (for she was purified from her uncleanness); and she returned unto her house. And the woman conceived; and she sent and told David, and said, I am with child. And David sent to Joab, saying, Send me Uriah the Hittite. And Joab sent Uriah to David. And when Uriah was come unto him, David asked of him how Joab did, and how the people fared, and how the war prospered. And David said to Uriah, Go down to thy house, and wash thy feet. And Uriah departed out of the king's house, and there followed him a mess of food from the king. But Uriah slept at the door of the king's house with all the servants of his lord, and went not down to his house. And when they had told David, saying, Uriah went not down unto his house, David said unto Uriah, Art thou not

100

come from a journey? wherefore didst thou not go down unto thy house? And Uriah said unto David, The ark, and Israel, and Judah, abide in booths; and my lord Joab, and the servants of my lord, are encamped in the open field; shall I then go into my house, to eat and to drink, and to lie with my wife? as thou livest, and as thy soul liveth, I will not do this thing. And David said to Uriah, Tarry here to-day also, and to-morrow I will let thee depart. So Uriah abode in Jerusalem that day, and the morrow. And when David had called him, he did eat and drink before him; and he made him drunk: and at even he went out to lie on his bed with the servants of his lord, but went not down to his house. And it came to pass in the morning, that David wrote a letter to Joab, and sent it by the hand of Uriah. And he wrote in the letter, saying, Set ye Uriah in the forefront of the hottest battle, and retire ye from him, that he may be smitten, and die. And it came to pass, when Joab kept watch upon the city, that he assigned Uriah unto the place where he knew that valiant men were. And the men of the city went out, and fought with Joab: and there fell some of the people, even of the servants of David; and Uriah the Hittite died also. Then Joab sent and told David all the things concerning the war; and he charged the messenger, saying, When thou hast made an end of telling all the things concerning the war unto the king, it shall be that, if the king's wrath arise, and he say unto thee, Wherefore went ye so nigh unto the city to fight? knew ye not that they would shoot from the wall? who smote Abimelech the son of Jerubbesheth? did not a woman cast an upper millstone upon him from the wall, so that he died at Thebez? why went ye so nigh the wall? then shalt thou say, Thy servant Uriah the Hittite is dead also. So the messenger went, and came and showed David all that Joab had sent him for. And the messenger said unto David, The men prevailed against us, and came out unto us into the field, and we were upon them even unto the entrance of the gate. And the shooters shot at thy servants from off the wall; and some of the king's servants are dead, and thy servant Uriah the Hittite is dead also."

Deuteronomy 13:1-4, "If there arise in the midst of thee a prophet, or a dreamer of dreams, and he give thee a sign or a wonder, and the sign or the wonder come to pass, whereof he spake unto thee, saying, Let us go after other gods, which thou hast not known, and let us serve them; thou shalt not hearken unto the words of that prophet, or unto that dreamer of dreams: for JEHOVAH your GOD proveth you, to know whether ye love JEHOVAH your GOD with all your heart and with all your soul. Ye shall walk after JEHOVAH your GOD, and fear HIM, and keep HIS commandments, and obey HIS voice, and ye shall serve HIM, and cleave unto HIM."

Ω

GOD does not want me to put faith in a place. Places have relevance, but at HIS discretion, their significance rises and falls. Jeremiah reminds the children of Israel of their previous misplaced faith in Shiloh. Jeremiah warned them because they were vulnerable to the same circumstances in Jerusalem.

A

Joshua 18:1-2, "And the whole congregation of the children of Israel assembled themselves together at Shiloh, and set up the tent of meeting there: and the land was subdued before them. And there remained among the children of Israel seven tribes, which had not yet divided their inheritance."

1 Samuel 4:1-11, "And the word of Samuel came to all Israel. And the Philistines put themselves in array against Israel: and when they joined battle, Israel was smitten before the Philistines; and they slew of the army in the field about four thousand men. And when the people were come into the camp, the elders of Israel said, Wherefore hath JEHOVAH smitten us to-day before the Philistines? Let us fetch the ark of the covenant of JEHOVAH out of Shiloh unto us, that it may come among us, and save us out of the hand of our enemies. So the people sent to Shiloh; and they brought from thence the ark of the covenant of JEHOVAH of hosts, WHO sitteth above the cherubim:

and the two sons of Eli (the high priest), Hophni and Phinehas, were there with the ark of the covenant of GOD. And when the ark of the covenant of JEHOVAH came into the camp, all Israel shouted with a great shout, so that the earth rang again. And when the Philistines heard the noise of the shout, they said, What meaneth the noise of this great shout in the camp of the Hebrews? And they understood that the ark of JEHOVAH was come into the camp. And the Philistines were afraid, for they said, GOD is come into the camp. And they said, Woe unto us! for there hath not been such a thing heretofore. Woe unto us! who shall deliver us out of the hand of these mighty gods? these are the gods that smote the Egyptians with all manner of plagues in the wilderness. Be strong, and quit yourselves like men, O ye Philistines, that ye be not servants unto the Hebrews, as they have been to you: quit yourselves like men, and fight. And the Philistines fought, and Israel was smitten, and they fled every man to his tent: and there was a very great slaughter; for there fell of Israel thirty thousand footmen. And the ark of GOD was taken; and the two sons of Eli, Hophni and Phinehas, were slain."

Jeremiah 7:12-15, "But go ye now unto my place which was in Shiloh, where I caused my name to dwell at the first, and see what I did to it for the wickedness of my people Israel. And now, because ye have done all these works, saith JEHOVAH, and I spake unto you, rising up early and speaking, but ye heard not; and I called you, but ye answered not: therefore will I do unto the house which is called by MY name, wherein ye trust, and unto the place which I gave to you and to your fathers, as I did to Shiloh. And I will cast you out of MY sight, as I have cast out all your brethren, even the whole seed of Ephraim."

Jeremiah 26:4-6, "And thou shalt say unto them, Thus saith JEHOVAH: If ye will not hearken to ME, to walk in MY law, which I have set before you, to hearken to the words of MY servants the prophets, whom I send unto you, even rising up early and sending them, but ye have not hearkened; then will I make this house like Shiloh, and will make this city a curse to all the nations of the earth."

Ω

Jeremiah preaches to the people in order to cause them to reflect on the outcome of Shiloh, because the same result was going to happen to Jerusalem. When deliverance is dire, my hopes must cling to JESUS. Deliverance is not that everything goes my way, but that JESUS secures my welfare. When I am attentive, I will take notice whether the LORD vindicates my cause, or if he disproves my methods to accomplish goals.

I once worked delivering appliances and televisions, and paid a commission per delivery. In the morning, I loaded my truck at the warehouse, and sometimes I had a return pickup from a customer's home. If I had to return an item, it was supposed to go to the store it was purchased, then I got a commission from that store. One morning my new manager informed me to make a return pickup, but bring it back to the warehouse. That voided my commission, and I was quite upset. I felt like I spent the whole day in frustrated talking to GOD until I thought maybe it is me, maybe I am wrong.

Then I prayed, "LORD, if I am wrong show me, and you have to make it plain, but if he is wrong show him." The next morning, I was unloading the item off my truck, and William Mitchell, a fellow senior driver, asked, "What are you doing?" My snappy response, "I'm doing what your boss told me to do." He said, "No, no, no. You're supposed to take that to the store." "I know that, and you know that, but this is what I was told to do," I explained.

He became more agitated than me as his upper torso and arm flailed like an old washing machine agitator. "Oooh! He's wrong for that," William pronounced. Bug-eyed as my oriental features mustered from seeing both William losing it and our boss walking behind him. "Where is he?!" William exclaimed. I tried to mouth to him with a slight whisper, "He's behind you." He looked at me with a questioning expression on his face.

I softly repeated, "He's behind you." He quickly composed himself, and turned around. Next, he put his right arm around the shoulders of our boss, and told him, "Mister ???, you were wrong for

104

doing that to this man," as his stretched out left arm pointed at me. I was beside myself as I walked to the open dock to find a private place to thank the LORD, and it did not matter that my commission was forfeited because I knew HE heard my prayer. Money is a temporary solution, but it is vain if HIS blessing is not in it.

A

Psalms 127:1' "Except JEHOVAH build the house, They labor in vain that build it: Except JEHOVAH keep the city, The watchman waketh but in vain."

Ω

Through history people have worshipped things that have been proven unfaithful. *The Holy Bible* is ripe with scripture concerning devotion to idols because of people's spiritual vulnerability to something tangible outside of oneself. Idol worship is a faith of deep insecurity that neither has the power to change circumstances, nor does it empower worshippers to change their behavior. Idol worshippers either willingly, or ignorantly succumb to their carnal nature as a result of powerlessness.

A

Genesis 35:1-5, "And GOD said unto Jacob, Arise, go up to Beth-el, and dwell there: and make there an altar unto GOD, WHO appeared unto thee when thou fleddest from the face of Esau thy brother. Then Jacob said unto his household, and to all that were with him, Put away the foreign gods that are among you, and purify yourselves, and change your garments: and let us arise, and go up to Beth-el; and I will make there an altar unto GOD, WHO answered me in the day of my distress, and was with me in the way which I went. And they gave unto Jacob all the foreign gods which were in their hand, and the rings which were in their ears; and Jacob hid them under the oak which was by Shechem. And they journeyed: and a terror of GOD was upon the cities that were round about them, and they did not pursue after the sons of Jacob."

Judges 18:1-31, "In those days there was no king in Israel: and in those days the tribe of the Danites sought them an inheritance to dwell in; for unto that day their inheritance had not fallen unto them among the tribes of Israel. And the children of Dan sent of their family five men from their whole number, men of valor, from Zorah, and from Eshtaol, to spy out the land, and to search it; and they said unto them, Go, search the land. And they came to the hill-country of Ephraim, unto the house of Micah, and lodged there. When they were by the house of Micah, they knew the voice of the young man the Levite; and they turned aside thither, and said unto him, Who brought thee hither? and what doest thou in this place? and what hast thou here? And he said unto them, Thus and thus hath Micah dealt with me, and he hath hired me, and I am become his priest. And they said unto him, Ask counsel, we pray thee, of GOD, that we may know whether our way which we go shall be prosperous. And the priest said unto them, Go in peace: before JEHOVAH is your way wherein ye go. Then the five men departed, and came to Laish, and saw the people that were therein, how they dwelt in security, after the manner of the Sidonians, quiet and secure; for there was none in the land, possessing authority, that might put them to shame in anything, and they were far from the Sidonians, and had no dealings with any man. And they came unto their brethren to Zorah and Eshtaol: and their brethren said unto them, What say ye? And they said, Arise, and let us go up against them; for we have seen the land, and, behold, it is very good: and are ye still? be not slothful to go and to enter in to possess the land. When ye go, ye shall come unto a people secure, and the land is large; for GOD hath given it into your hand, a place where there is no want of anything that is in the earth. And there set forth from thence of the family of the Danites, out of Zorah and out of Eshtaol, six hundred men girt with weapons of war. And they went up, and encamped in Kiriath-jearim, in Judah: wherefore they called that place Mahaneh-dan, unto this day; behold, it is behind Kiriath-jearim. And they passed thence

106

unto the hill-country of Ephraim, and came unto the house of Micah. Then answered the five men that went to spy out the country of Laish, and said unto their brethren, Do ye know that there is in these houses an ephod, and teraphim, and a graven image, and a molten image? now therefore consider what ye have to do. And they turned aside thither, and came to the house of the young man the Levite, even unto the house of Micah, and asked him of his welfare. And the six hundred men girt with their weapons of war, who were of the children of Dan, stood by the entrance of the gate. And the five men that went to spy out the land went up, and came in thither, and took the graven image, and the ephod, and the teraphim, and the molten image: and the priest stood by the entrance of the gate with the six hundred men girt with weapons of war. And when these went into Micah's house, and fetched the graven image, the ephod, and the teraphim, and the molten image, the priest said unto them, What do ye? And they said unto him, Hold thy peace, lay thy hand upon thy mouth, and go with us, and be to us a father and a priest: is it better for thee to be priest unto the house of one man, or to be priest unto a tribe and a family in Israel? And the priest's heart was glad, and he took the ephod, and the teraphim, and the graven image, and went in the midst of the people. So they turned and departed, and put the little ones and the cattle and the goods before them. When they were a good way from the house of Micah, the men that were in the houses near to Micah's house were gathered together, and overtook the children of Dan. And they cried unto the children of Dan. And they turned their faces, and said unto Micah, What aileth thee, that thou comest with such a company? And he said, ye have taken away my gods which I made, and the priest, and are gone away, and what have I more? and how then say ye unto me, What aileth thee? And the children of Dan said unto him, Let not thy voice be heard among us, lest angry fellows fall upon you, and thou lose thy life, with the lives of thy household. And the children of Dan went their way: and when Micah saw that they were too strong for him, he turned and went back unto his house. And they took that which Micah had made, and the priest whom he had, and came unto Laish, unto a people quiet and secure, and smote them with the edge of the sword; and they burnt the city with fire. And there was no deliverer, because it was far from Sidon, and they had no dealings with any man; and it was in the valley that lieth by Beth-rehob. And they built the city, and dwelt therein. And they called the name of the city Dan, after the name of Dan their father, who was born unto Israel: howbeit the name of the city was Laish at the first. And the children of Dan set up for themselves the graven image: and Jonathan, the son of Gershom, the son of Moses, he and his sons were priests to the tribe of the Danites until the day of the captivity of the land. So they set them up Micah's graven image which he made, all the time that the house of GOD was in Shiloh."

2 Kings 17:7-17, "And it was so, because the children of Israel had sinned against JEHOVAH their GOD, WHO brought them up out of the land of Egypt from under the hand of Pharaoh king of Egypt, and had feared other gods, and walked in the statutes of the nations, whom JEHOVAH cast out from before the children of Israel, and of the kings of Israel, which they made. And the children of Israel did secretly things that were not right against JEHOVAH their GOD: and they built them high places in all their cities, from the tower of the watchmen to the fortified city; and they set them up pillars and Asherim upon every high hill, and under every green tree; and there they burnt incense in all the high places, as did the nations whom JEHOVAH carried away before them; and they wrought wicked things to provoke JEHOVAH to anger; and they served idols, whereof JEHOVAH had said unto them, Ye shall not do this thing. Yet JEHOVAH testified unto Israel, and unto Judah, by every prophet, and every seer, saying, Turn ye from your evil ways, and keep MY commandments and MY statutes, according to all the law which I commanded your fathers, and which I sent to you by MY servants the prophets. Notwithstanding, they would not hear, but hardened their neck, like to the neck of their fathers, who believed not in JEHOVAH their GOD. And they rejected HIS statutes, and HIS covenant that HE made with their fathers, and HIS testimonies which HE testified unto them; and they followed vanity, and became vain, and went after the nations that were round about them, concerning whom JEHOVAH had charged them that they should not do like them. And they forsook all the commandments of JEHOVAH their GOD, and made them molten images, even two calves, and made an Asherah, and worshipped all the host of heaven, and served Baal. And they caused their sons and their daughters to pass through the fire, and used divination and enchantments, and sold themselves to do that which was evil in the sight of JEHOVAH, to provoke HIM to anger."

Ω

The faithfulness of my GOD, stirs a well of praise and victory to those who are faithful to HIM. Praise is the natural result from identifying GOD's faithful sovereignty. HE is faithful to accomplish the good work HE has begun in me.

A

Exodus 15:1-19, "Then sang Moses and the children of Israel this song unto JEHOVAH, and spake, saying, I will sing unto JEHOVAH, for HE hath triumphed gloriously: The horse and his rider hath HE thrown into the sea. JEHOVAH is my strength and song, And HE is become my salvation: This is my GOD, and I will praise HIM; My father's GOD, and I will exalt HIM. JEHOVAH is a man of war: JEHOVAH is HIS name. Pharaoh's chariots and his host hath HE cast into the sea; And his chosen captains are sunk in the Red Sea. The deeps cover them: They went down into the depths like a stone. THY right hand, O JEHOVAH, is glorious in power, THY right hand, O JEHOVAH, dasheth in pieces the enemy. And in the greatness of THINE excellency THOU overthrowest them that rise up against THEE: THOU sendest forth THY wrath, it consumeth them as stubble. And with the blast of THY nostrils the waters were piled up, The floods stood upright as a heap; The deeps were congealed in the heart of the sea. The enemy said, I will pursue, I will overtake, I will divide the spoil; My desire shall be satisfied upon them; I will draw my sword, my hand shall destroy them. THOU didst blow with THY wind, the sea covered them: They sank as lead in the mighty waters.

Who is like unto THEE, O JEHOVAH, among the gods? Who is like THEE, glorious in holiness, Fearful in praises, doing wonders? THOU stretchedst out THY right hand, The earth swallowed them. THOU in THY lovingkindness hast led the people that THOU hast redeemed: THOU hast guided them in THY strength to THY holy habitation. The peoples have heard, they tremble: Pangs have taken hold on the inhabitants of Philistia. Then were the chiefs of Edom dismayed; The mighty men of Moab, trembling taketh hold upon them: All the inhabitants of Canaan are melted away. Terror and dread falleth upon them; By the greatness of THINE arm they are as still as a stone; Till THY people pass over, O JEHOVAH, Till the people pass over that THOU hast purchased. THOU wilt bring them in, and plant them in the mountain of THINE inheritance, The place, O JEHOVAH, which THOU hast made for THEE to dwell in, The sanctuary, O LORD, which THY hands have established. JEHOVAH shall reign for ever and ever. For the horses of Pharaoh went in with his chariots and with his horsemen into the sea, and JEHOVAH brought back the waters of the sea upon them; but the children of Israel walked on dry land in the midst of the sea."

Psalms 20:5-9, "We will triumph in THY salvation, And in the name of our GOD we will set up our banners: JEHOVAH fulfil all thy petitions. Now know I that JEHOVAH saveth HIS anointed; HE will answer HIM from HIS holy heaven With the saving strength of HIS right hand. Some trust in chariots, and some in horses; But we will make mention of the name of JEHOVAH our GOD. Save, JEHOVAH: Let the KING answer us when we call."

Psalms 33:16-20, "There is no king saved by the multitude of a host: A mighty man is not delivered by great strength. A horse is a vain thing for safety; Neither doth he deliver any by his great power. Behold, the eye of JEHOVAH is upon them that fear HIM, Upon them that hope in HIS lovingkindness; To deliver their soul from death, And to keep them alive in famine. Our soul hath waited for JEHOVAH: HE is our help and our shield."

Ω

GOD is all about follow through, so much so that HE has perfected it. HE gives me multiple chances to be faithful, not vice versa. Notice that Moses states when, not if these things will come to pass.

A

Deuteronomy 17:14-17, "When thou art come unto the land which JEHOVAH thy GOD giveth thee, and shalt possess it, and shalt dwell therein, and shalt say, I will set a king over me, like all the nations that are round about me; thou shalt surely set him king over thee, whom JEHOVAH thy GOD shall choose: one from among thy brethren shalt thou set king over thee; thou mayest not put a foreigner over thee, who is not thy brother. Only he shall not multiply horses to himself, nor cause the people to return to Egypt, to the end that he may multiply horses; forasmuch as JEHOVAH hath said unto you, Ye shall henceforth return no more that way. Neither shall he multiply wives to himself, that his heart turn not away: neither shall he greatly multiply to himself silver and gold."

Ω

GOD is **always** ready to be faithful. HE is waiting for me to figure that out. In order to be faithful to GOD I must be willing to sacrifice myself, and what I feel entitled. Faithfulness requires my initial sacrifice to HIM in order to connect with identifying HIM first as scripture states.

A

Genesis 4:4-5, "And Abel, he also brought of the firstlings of his flock and of the fat thereof. And JEHOVAH had respect unto Abel and to his offering: but unto Cain and to his offering HE had not respect. And Cain was very wroth, and his countenance fell."

111

Psalms 15:1-5, "JEHOVAH, who shall sojourn in thy tabernacle? Who shall dwell in thy holy hill? He that walketh uprightly, and worketh righteousness, And speaketh truth in his heart; He that slandereth not with his tongue, Nor doeth evil to his friend, Nor taketh up a reproach against his neighbor; In whose eyes a reprobate is despised, But who honoreth them that fear JEHOVAH; He that sweareth to his own hurt, and changeth not; He that putteth not out his money to interest, Nor taketh reward against the innocent. He that doeth these things shall never be moved."

Luke 6:27-36, (JESUS speaking) "But I say unto you that hear, Love your enemies, do good to them that hate you, bless them that curse you, pray for them that despitefully use you. To him that smiteth thee on the one cheek offer also the other; and from him that taketh away thy cloak withhold not thy coat also. Give to every one that asketh thee; and of him that taketh away thy goods ask them not again. And as ye would that men should do to you, do ye also to them likewise. And if ye love them that love you, what thank have ye? for even sinners love those that love them. And if ye do good to them that do good to you, what thank have ye? for even sinners do the same. And if ye lend to them of whom ye hope to receive, what thank have ye? even sinners lend to sinners, to receive again as much. But love your enemies, and do them good, and lend, never despairing; and your reward shall be great, and ye shall be sons of the MOST HIGH: for HE is kind toward the unthankful and evil. Be ye merciful, even as your FATHER is merciful."

Ω

Calamity **always** follows unfaithful decisions against GOD's instructions. HE warns me of the coming calamity from my disobedience. GOD is not winding up for an "I told you so," but HIS goal is to prevent a life of regrets. The children of Israel were warned not to return to Egypt for help, but did it anyway.

Deuteronomy 17:16, "Only he shall not multiply horses to himself, nor cause the people to return to Egypt, to the end that he may multiply horses; forasmuch as JEHOVAH hath said unto you, **Ye shall henceforth return no more that way.**"

Isaiah 30:1-3, "Woe to the rebellious children, saith JEHOVAH, that take counsel, but not of ME; and that make a league, but not of MY SPIRIT, that they may add sin to sin, that set out to go down into Egypt, and have not asked at MY mouth; to strengthen themselves in the strength of Pharaoh, and to take refuge in the shadow of Egypt! Therefore shall the strength of Pharaoh be your shame, and the refuge in the shadow of Egypt your confusion."

Isaiah 31:1-3, "Woe to them that go down to Egypt for help, and rely on horses, and trust in chariots because they are many, and in horsemen because they are very strong, but they look not unto the HOLY ONE of Israel, neither seek JEHOVAH! Yet HE also is wise, and will bring evil, and will not call back HIS words, but will arise against the house of the evil-doers, and against the help of them that work iniquity. Now the Egyptians are men, and not GOD; and their horses flesh, and not spirit: and when JEHOVAH shall stretch out HIS hand, both he that helpeth shall stumble, and he that is helped shall fall, and they all shall be consumed together."

Jeremiah 37:4-10, "Now Jeremiah came in and went out among the people; for they had not put him into prison. And Pharaoh's army was come forth out of Egypt; and when the Chaldeans that were besieging Jerusalem heard tidings of them, they brake up from Jerusalem. Then came the WORD of JEHOVAH unto the prophet Jeremiah, saying, Thus saith JEHOVAH, the GOD of Israel, Thus shall ye say to the king of Judah, that sent you unto ME to inquire of ME: Behold, Pharaoh's army, which is come forth to help you, shall return to Egypt into their own land. And the Chaldeans shall come again, and fight against this city; and they shall take it, and burn it with fire. Thus saith JEHOVAH, Deceive not yourselves, saying, The Chaldeans shall surely depart from us; for they shall not depart. For though ye had smitten the whole army of the Chaldeans that fight against you, and there remained but wounded men among them, yea would they rise up every man in his tent, and burn this city with fire."

Jeremiah 43:2-7, "then spake Azariah the son of Hoshaiah, and Johanan the son of Kareah, and all the proud men, saying unto Jeremiah, Thou speakest falsely: JEHOVAH our GOD hath not sent thee to say, Ye shall not go into Egypt to sojourn there; but Baruch the son of Neriah setteth thee on against us, to deliver us into the hand of the Chaldeans, that they may put us to death, and carry us away captive to Babylon. So Johanan the son of Kareah, and all the captains of the forces, and all the people, obeyed not the voice of JEHOVAH, to dwell in the land of Judah. But Johanan the son of Kareah, and all the captains of the forces, took all the remnant of Judah, that were returned from all the nations whither they had been driven, to sojourn in the land of Judah; the men, and the women, and the children, and the king's daughters, and every person that Nebuzaradan the captain of the guard had left with Gedaliah the son of Ahikam, the son of Shaphan; and Jeremiah the prophet, and Baruch the son of Neriah; and they came into the land of Egypt; for they obeyed not the voice of JEHOVAH: and they came unto Tahpanhes."

$$\Omega$$

GOD longs for me to submit to HIS WORD because HE does not fail, and all my strength of will has to comply, even if the outcome appears contrary to my benefit. If HE picks up the pieces of my broken life when I am unfaithful and repent, then what do I have to lose from being faithful. Being faithful requires knowing my complete dependence on HIM to make life functional.

FELLOWSHIP

Chapter 10

Relationship is a motivator for GOD, and HIS engagement in fellowshipping with flawed sentient beings proves HIS will has room for me. Everything GOD does is for someone else's benefit. While JESUS was present on earth, HE engaged with Jews, gentiles, rich, poor, friendly, defiant, young, and old. HE made himself available to any willing soul.

GOD, WHO is self-sufficient, does not have need or dependence for anything. Then why does HE involve HIMSELF with fallible people like me? Fellowship. GOD loves people. Abram was a pagan for up to seventy-five years.

Isaac lied, he failed to protect his wife from a potentially aggressive man, who desired her, but he has fellowship with GOD. Isaac favored his son Esau more than his son Jacob, but GOD cultivated a relationship with Jacob, even though Jacob was a complicit deceiver. The sons of Jacob conspired to harm their brother, Joseph, and are known as the tribes of Israel through fellowship with GOD. Joseph married a pagan woman, and maintains fellowship with GOD.

A

Genesis 12:4, "So Abram went, as JEHOVAH had spoken unto him; and Lot went with him: and Abram was seventy and five years old when he departed out of Haran."

Genesis 26:7, "And the men of the place asked him (Isaac) of his wife. And he said, She is my sister. For he feared to say, My wife. Lest, said he, the men of the place should kill me for Rebekah. Because she was fair to look upon."

Genesis 25:28, "Now Isaac loved Esau, because he did eat of his venison. And Rebekah loved Jacob."

Genesis 27:1-29, "And it came to pass, that when Isaac was old, and his eyes were dim, so that he could not see, he called Esau his elder son, and said unto him, My son. And he said unto him, Here am I. And he said, Behold now, I am old, I know not the day of my death. Now therefore take, I pray thee, thy weapons, thy quiver and thy bow, and go out to the field, and take me venison. And make me savory food, such as I love, and bring it to me, that I may eat. That my soul may bless thee before I die. And Rebekah heard when Isaac spake to Esau his son. And Esau went to the field to hunt for venison, and to bring it. And Rebekah spake unto Jacob her son, saying, Behold, I heard thy father speak unto Esau thy brother, saying, Bring me venison, and make me savory food, that I may eat, and bless thee before JEHOVAH before my death. Now therefore, my son, obey my voice according to that which I command thee. Go now to the flock, and fetch me from thence two good kids of the goats. And I will make them savory food for thy father, such as he loveth. And thou shalt bring it to thy father, that he may eat, so that he may bless thee before his death. And Jacob said to Rebekah his mother, Behold, Esau my brother is a hairy man, and I am a smooth man. My father peradventure will feel me, and I shall seem to him as a deceiver. And I shall bring a curse upon me, and not a blessing. And his mother said unto him, Upon me be thy curse, my son. Only obey my voice, and go fetch me them. And he went, and fetched, and brought them to his mother. And his mother made savory food, such as his father loved. And Rebekah took the goodly garments of Esau her elder son, which were with her in the house, and put them upon Jacob her younger son. And she put the skins of the kids of the goats upon his hands, and upon the smooth of his neck. And she gave the savory food and the bread, which she had prepared, into the hand of her son Jacob. And he came unto his father, and said, My father. And he said, Here am I. Who art thou, my son? And Jacob said unto his father, I am Esau thy first-born; I have done according as thou badest me: arise, I pray thee, sit and eat of my venison, that thy soul may bless me. And Isaac said unto his son, How is it that thou hast found it so quickly, my son? And he said, Because JEHOVAH thy GOD sent me good speed. And Isaac said unto Jacob, Come near, I pray thee, that I may feel thee, my son, whether thou be my very son Esau or not. And Jacob went near unto Isaac his father. And he felt him, and said, The voice is Jacob's voice, but the hands are the hands of Esau. And he discerned him not, because his hands were hairy, as his brother Esau's hands. So he blessed him. And he said, Art thou my very son Esau? And he said, I am. And he said, Bring it near to me, and I will eat of my son's venison, that my soul may bless thee. And he brought it near to him, and he did eat. And he brought him wine, and he drank. And his father Isaac said unto him, Come near now, and kiss me, my son. And he came near, and kissed him. And he smelled the smell of his raiment, and blessed him, and said, See, the smell of my son is as the smell of a field which JEHOVAH hath blessed. And GOD give thee of the dew of heaven, And of the fatness of the earth, And plenty of grain and new wine. Let peoples serve thee, And nations bow down to thee. Be lord over thy brethren, And let thy mother's sons bow down to thee. Cursed be every one that curseth thee, And blessed be every one that blesseth thee."

Genesis 37:18-27, "And they (the brothers of Joseph) saw him (Joseph) afar off, and before he came near unto them, they conspired against him to slay him. And they said one to another, Behold, this dreamer cometh. Come now therefore, and let us slay him, and cast him into one of the pits, and we will say, And evil beast hath devoured him: and we shall see what will become of his dreams. And Reuben heard it, and delivered him out of their hand, and said, Let us not take his life. And Reuben said unto them, Shed no blood; cast him into this pit that is in the wilderness, but lay no hand upon him: that he might deliver him out of their hand, to restore him to his father. And it came to pass, when Joseph was come unto his brethren, that they stripped Joseph of his coat, the coat of many colors that was on him; and they took him, and cast him into the pit: and the pit was empty, there was no water in it. And they sat down to eat bread: and they lifted up their eyes and looked, and, behold, a caravan of Ishmaelites was coming from Gilead, with their camels bearing spicery and balm and myrrh, going to carry it down to Egypt. And Judah said unto his brethren, What profit is it if we slay our brother and conceal his blood? Come, and let us sell him to the Ishmaelites, and let not our hand be upon him; for he is our brother, our flesh. And his brethren hearkened unto him."

Genesis 41:45, "And Pharaoh called Joseph's name Zaphenath-paneah; and he gave him to wife Asenath, the daughter of Poti-phera priest of On. And Joseph went out over the land of Egypt."

Ω

Moses murdered an Egyptian, and found fellowship with GOD. Aaron, the high priest, made an idol for Israel to worship, but has fellowship with GOD. Again, GOD loves people, and HE desires me to do the same even though I am flawed.

A

Exodus 2:11-12, "And it came to pass in those days, when Moses was grown up, that he went out unto his brethren, and looked on their burdens: and he saw an Egyptian smiting a Hebrew, one of his breth-ren. And he looked this way and that way, and when he saw that there was no man, he smote the Egyptian, and hid him in the sand."

Exodus 32:1-6, "And when the people saw that Moses delayed to come down from the mount, the people gathered themselves together unto Aaron, and said unto him, Up, make us gods, which shall go before us; for as for this Moses, the man that brought us up out of the land of Egypt, we know not what is become of him. And Aaron said unto them, Break off the golden rings, which are in the ears of your wives, of your sons, and of your daughters, and bring them unto me. And all the people brake off the golden rings which were in their ears, and brought them unto Aaron. And he received it at their hand, and fashioned it with a graving tool, and made it a molten calf: and they said, These are thy gods, O Israel, which brought thee up out of the land of Egypt. And when Aaron saw this, he built an altar before it;

118

and Aaron made proclamation, and said, To-morrow shall be a feast to JEHOVAH. And they rose up early on the morrow, and offered burnt-offerings, and brought peace-offerings; and the people sat down to eat and to drink, and rose up to play."

Ω

When I repent, GOD **always** forgives my sin (with the unique exception to the sin of blasphemy against the HOLY SPIRIT) in order to restore fellowship, and according to JESUS heaven rejoices when I repent. Fellowship is the primary reason for repentance, and heaven rejoices because of the restoration of my relationship with GOD. The restoration of my relationship with GOD acknowledges HIM as LORD, and notifies heaven that I am yielding to the greatness of WHO HE is.

A

Luke 15:7, (JESUS speaking) "I say unto you, that even so there shall be joy in heaven over one sinner that repenteth, more than over ninety and nine righteous persons, who need no repentance."

Ω

I am able to read the story of my Bible heroes progression of faith, but I have to live mine. Since holy, holy, holy GOD is willing to have fellowship with them, I need to do the same with sincere people I do not necessarily agree with on all aspects, but who are compelled to find GOD. The only way to experience more abundance in life is being a part of the experiences of other people. When friends talk about shared experiences, emotions go deeper, higher, and farther than reminiscing alone.

I neither have the same environment, nor personality as biblical heroes, but GOD desires a fellowship with me, and that entails my own variety of experiences, quarks, and flaws. JESUS shared life in order to teach me to share life. Think about it, did he really need disciples? To preach, to heal, to perform miracles, or to raise the dead, but life is always more exciting in a team. Members of a team have different points of view, different perspectives, different personalities, but victory has the same sweet savor.

The position I have in CHRIST is not necessarily my position on earth, which means that I am to be ruled by GOD, and subjugate to man's authority. My relationships with people reflect my relationship with GOD, and I must be mindful that this is HIS view. Armed with the knowledge of what GOD values, I am empowered to make faithful decisions that enable GOD to fight for me instead of me struggling alone. When life seems to depress me, it is not time to end my fellowship with GOD, for HE is progressing our relationship into a friendship as described by JESUS.

A

John 15:12-17, (JESUS speaking) "This is MY commandment, that ye love one another, even as I have loved you. Greater love hath no man than this, that a man lay down his life for his friends. Ye are MY friends, if ye do the things which I command you. No longer do I call you servants; for the servant knoweth not what his lord doeth: but I have called you friends; for all things that I heard from MY FATHER, I have made known unto you. Ye did not choose ME, but I chose you, and appointed you, that ye should go and bear fruit, and that your fruit should abide: that whatsoever ye shall ask of the FATHER in MY name, HE may give it you. These things I command you, that ye may love one another."

Ω

The better I understand my relationship with GOD I can fulfill my role as a disciple. I am a disciple first, and GOD determines the elevation of my role in both HIS view and the world's view. When I yield to HIM, my position in this world is what, when, and where HE desires me. Because GOD reveals HIS actions to HIS friends, I am not going to miss HIS desire for me.

A

Genesis 18:17-33, "And JEHOVAH said, Shall I hide from Abraham that which I do; seeing that Abraham had surely become a great and mighty nation, and all the nations of the earth shall be blessed in him? For I have known him, to the end that he may command his children and his household after him, that they may keep the way of JEHOVAH, to do righteousness and justice; to the end that JEHO-VAH may bring upon Abraham that which HE hath spoken of him. And JEHOVAH said, Because the cry of Sodom and Gomorrah is great, and because their sin is very grievous; I will go down now, and see whether they have done altogether according to the cry of it, which is come unto ME; and if not, I will know. And the men turned from thence, and went toward Sodom: but Abraham stood yet before JEHOVAH. And Abraham drew near, and said, Wilt thou consume the righteous with the wicked? Peradventure there are fifty righteous within the city: wilt THOU consume and not spare the place for the fifty righteous that are therein? That be far from THEE to do after this manner, to slay the righteous with the wicked, that so the right-eous should be as the wicked; that be far from THEE: shall not the JUDGE of all the earth do right? And JEHOVAH said, If I find in Sodom fifty righteous within the city, then I will spare all the place for their sake. And Abraham answered and said, Behold now, I have taken upon me to speak unto the LORD, who am but dust and ashes: peradventure there shall lack five of the fifty righteous: wilt THOU destroy all the city for lack of five? And he said, I will not destroy it, if I find there forty and five. And he spake unto HIM yet again, and said, Peradventure there shall be forty found there. And HE said, I will not do it for the forty's sake. And he said, Oh let not the LORD be angry, and I will speak: peradventure there shall thirty be found there. And HE said, I will not do it, if I find thirty there. And he said,

Behold now, I have taken upon me to speak unto the LORD: peradventure there shall be twenty found there. And HE said, I will not destroy it for the twenty's sake. And he said, Oh let not the LORD be angry, and I will speak yet but this once: peradventure ten shall be found there. And HE said, I will not destroy it for the ten's sake. And JEHOVAH went HIS way, as soon as HE had left off communing with Abraham: and Abraham returned unto his place."

Ω

My fellowship with GOD provides opportunities as HIS WORD states. Having fellowship with GOD does not mean GOD entitles me to do whatever I want. HE may refuse me things I desire, even if that desire has a positive disposition. Just as GOD instructed David not to build HIM a house (sanctuary) because of David's previous actions.

A

Revelation 3:7, (JESUS speaking) "And to the angel of the church in Philadelphia write: These things saith HE that is holy, HE that is true, HE that hath the key of David, HE that openeth and none shall shut, and that shutteth and none openeth:"

1 Chronicles 28:2-3, "Then David the king stood up upon his feet, and said, Hear me, my brethren, and my people: as for me, it was in my heart to build a house of rest for the ark of the covenant of JEHOVAH, and for the footstool of our GOD; and I had made ready for the building. But GOD said unto me, Thou shalt not build a house for MY name, because thou art a man of war, and hast shed blood."

Ω

GOD shows me that the way I treat people is the way I treat HIM, and the way I treat others is the way HE is going to allow people

122

to treat me. GOD evaluates my love for HIM based on my treatment of others, and my relationship with GOD elevates as HE judges the sincerity of my love for HIM. I am comfortable knowing some people are closer to GOD than I am, and that I do not have all the answers, but I am aware of HIS love for me. When I think of the prayers HE has answered, I am overwhelmed.

The GOD of the universe has other things to preoccupy HIS time, but HE chooses to affirm fellowship by acknowledging my prayers. HE will not forsake me, and is committed to the relationship between HE and I. GOD allows our relationship mature at my pace.

A

Matthew 25:31-46, (JESUS speaking) "But when the SON of man shall come in HIS glory, and all the angels with HIM, then shall HE sit on the throne of HIS glory: and before HIM shall be gathered all the nations: and HE shall separate them one from another, as the SHEPHERD separateth the sheep from the goats; and HE shall set the sheep on HIS right hand, but the goats on the left. Then shall the KING say unto them on HIS right hand, Come, ye blessed of MY FATHER, inherit the kingdom prepared for you from the foundation of the world: for I was hungry, and ye gave ME to eat; I was thirsty, and ye gave ME drink; I was a stranger, and ye took ME in; naked, and ye clothed ME; I was sick, and ye visited ME; I was in prison, and ye came unto ME. Then shall the righteous answer HIM, saying, LORD, when saw we THEE hungry, and fed THEE? or athirst, and gave THEE drink? And when saw we THEE a stranger, and took THEE in? or naked, and clothed THEE? And when saw we THEE sick, or in prison, and came unto THEE? And the KING shall answer and say unto them, Verily I say unto you, Inasmuch as ye did it unto one of these MY brethren, Then shall HE say also unto them on the left hand, Depart from ME, ye cursed, into the eternal fire which is prepared for the devil and his angels: for I was hungry, and ye did not give ME to eat; I was thirsty, and ye gave ME no drink; I was a stranger, and ye took ME not in; naked, and ye clothed ME not; sick, and in prison, and ye visited ME not. Then shall they also answer, saying, LORD, when saw we THEE hungry, or athirst, or a stranger, or naked, or sick, or in prison, and did not minister unto THEE? Then shall HE answer them, saying, Verily I say unto you, Inasmuch as ye did it not unto one of these least, ye did it not unto ME. And these shall go away into eternal punishment: but the righteous into eternal life."

Hebrews 13:1-3, "Let love of the brethren continue. Forget not to show love unto strangers: for thereby some have entertained angels unawares. Remember them that are in bonds, as bound with them; them that are ill-treated, as being yourselves also in the body."

1 John 4:20-21, "If a man say, I love GOD, and hateth his brother, he is a liar: for he that loveth not his brother whom he hath seen, cannot love GOD WHOM he hath not seen. And this commandment have we from HIM, that he who loveth GOD love his brother also."

Deuteronomy 31:1-6, "And Moses went and spake these words unto all Israel. And he said unto them, I am a hundred and twenty years old this day; I can no more go out and come in: and JEHOVAH hath said unto me, Thou shalt not go over this Jordan. JEHOVAH thy GOD, HE will go over before thee; HE will destroy these nations from before thee, and thou shalt dispossess them: And JEHOVAH will do unto them as HE did to Sihon and to Og, the kings of the Amorites, and unto their land; whom HE destroyed. And JEHOVAH will deliver them up before you, and ye shall do unto them according unto all the commandment which I have commanded you. Be strong and of good courage, fear not, nor be affrighted at them: for JEHOVAH thy GOD, HE it is that doth go with thee; HE will not fail thee, nor forsake thee."

Hebrews 13:5, "Be ye free from the love of money; content with such things as ye have: for HIMSELF (GOD) hath said, I will in no wise fail thee, neither will I in any wise forsake thee."

Ω

I talk to GOD about many issues, hopes, things I think are funny, artistic, and interesting. GOD allows me to gain insight into our conversations over time. HE responds to things I have talked to HIM about that I had forgotten like provisions for my family. HE remembers the prayers of my youth, and my heart has been stolen away by HIS kindnesses towards me, and those I love.

A

Psalms 37:3-7, "Trust in JEHOVAH, and do good; Dwell in the land, and feed on HIS faithfulness. Delight thyself also in JEHOVAH; And HE will give thee the desires of thy heart. Commit thy way unto JEHOVAH; Trust also in HIM, and HE will bring it to pass. And HE will make thy righteousness to go forth as the light, And thy justice as the noon-day. Rest in JEHOVAH, and wait patiently for HIM: Fret not thyself because of him who prospereth in his way, Because of the man who bringeth wicked devices to pass."

Ω

HIS love is constantly reinvigorating itself in ways I never dared to hope. I have witnessed GOD bless my family, and it brings me overwhelming joy. My children get the opportunity to fellowship with my GOD, and their GOD.

WISDOM

Chapter 10

Wisdom provides the ability to discern forthcoming events that are in a protracted view. As a practical matter, it is possible to have wisdom, but miss on understanding. Understanding allows me to grasp knowledge of the vision of wisdom, and then enact an application whether to halt or proceed. Fortunately, *The Holy Bible* instructs me that by fearing GOD I obtain wisdom, and understanding is in conjunction with obedience.

A

Psalm 111:10, "The fear of JEHOVAH is the beginning of wisdom; A good understanding have all they that do HIS commandments: HIS praise endureth for ever."

Proverbs 9:7-10, "He that correcteth a scoffer getteth to himself reviling; And he that reproveth a wicked man getteth himself a blot. Reprove not a scoffer, lest he hate thee: Reprove a wise man, and he will love thee. Give instruction to a wise man, and he will be yet wiser: Teach a righteous man, and he will increase in learning. The fear of JEHOVAH is the beginning of wisdom; And the knowledge of the HOLY ONE is understanding."

Ω

The book of *James* shares with me how to gain wisdom through prayer like Solomon. James' knowledge is from Solomon's example. GOD blessed Solomon because of his noble request, and then cycled blessings through the wisdom HE supplied.

A

James 1:5, "But if any of you lacketh wisdom, let him ask of GOD, WHO giveth to all liberally and upbraideth not; and it shall be given him."

1 Kings 3:5-12, "In Gibeon JEHOVAH appeared to Solomon in a dream by night; and GOD said, Ask what I shall give thee. And Solomon said, Thou hast showed unto THY servant David my father great lovingkindness, according as he walked before THEE in truth, and in righteousness, and in uprightness of heart with THEE; and THOU hast kept for him this great lovingkindness, that THOU hast given him a son to sit on his throne, as it is this day. And now, O JEHOVAH my GOD, THOU hast made THY servant king instead of David my father: and I am but a little child; I know not how to go out or come in. And THY servant is in the midst of THY people which THOU hast chosen, a great people, that cannot be numbered nor counted for multitude. Give THY servant therefore an understanding heart to judge THY people, that I may discern between good and evil; for who is able to judge this THY great people? And the speech pleased the LORD, that Solomon had asked this thing. And GOD said unto him, Because thou hast asked this thing, and hast not asked for thyself long life, neither hast asked riches for thyself, nor hast asked the life of thine enemies, but hast asked for thyself understanding to discern justice; behold, I have done according to thy word: lo, I have given thee a wise and an understanding heart; so that there hath been none like thee before thee, neither after thee shall any arise like unto thee."

Ω

GOD allows both just and unjust to prosper through wisdom. Higher education will grant a type wisdom, but success may prove elusive because education does not change the inner person. Wisdom is neither a necessity for salvation, nor is wisdom a guarantee to salvation; however, scripture makes it comparable to faith.

Proverbs 3:13-18, "Happy is the man that findeth wisdom, And the man that getteth understanding. For the gaining of it is better than the gaining of silver, And the profit thereof than fine gold. She is more precious than rubies: And none of the things thou canst desire are to be compared unto her. Length of days is in her right hand; In her left hand are riches and honor. Her ways are ways of pleasantness, And all her paths are peace. She is a tree of life to them that lay hold upon her: And happy is every one that retaineth her."

Proverbs 8:1-21, "Doth not wisdom cry, And understanding put forth her voice? On the top of high places by the way, Where the paths meet, she standeth; Beside the gates, at the entry of the city, At the coming in at the doors, she crieth aloud: Unto you, O men, I call; And my voice is to the sons of men. O ye simple, understand prudence; And, ye fools, be of an understanding heart. Hear, for I will speak excellent things; And the opening of my lips shall be right things. For my mouth shall utter truth; And wickedness is an abomination to my lips. All the words of my mouth are in righteousness; There is nothing crooked or perverse in them. They are all plain to him that understandeth, And right to them that find knowledge. Receive my instruction, and not silver; And knowledge rather than choice gold. For wisdom is better than rubies; And all the things that may be desired are not to be compared unto it. I wisdom have made prudence my dwelling, And find out knowledge and discretion. The fear of JEHOVAH is to hate evil: Pride, and arrogancy, and the evil way, And the perverse mouth, do I hate. Counsel is MINE, and sound knowledge: I am understanding; I have might. By ME kings reign, And princes decree justice. By ME princes rule, And nobles, even all the judges of the earth. I love them that love ME; And those that seek ME diligently shall find ME. Riches and honor are with ME; Yea, durable wealth and righteousness. MY fruit is better than gold, yea, than fine gold;

And MY revenue than choice silver. I walk in the way of righteousness, In the midst of the paths of justice; That I may cause those that
love ME to inherit substance, And that I may fill their treasuries."

1 Peter 1:7, "that the proof of your faith, being more precious than
gold that perisheth though it is proved by fire, may be found unto
praise and glory and honor at the revelation of JESUS CHRIST:"

Ω

Both Ahithophel and Solomon experienced the highs and
lows of wisdom. Ahithophel is an example of wisdom, but his ambition to achieve a more prominent position in Absalom's administra-
tion rather than being faithful to King David, lead him astray. Solomon had wisdom, but he became consumed by wealth and passion.

A

2 Samuel 15:12, "And Absalom sent for Ahithophel the Gilonite, David's counsellor, from his city, even from Giloh, while he was offering the sacrifices. And the conspiracy was strong; for the people increased continually with Absalom."

2 Samuel 15:31-34, "And one told David, saying, Ahithophel is
among the conspirators with Absalom. And David said, O
JEHOVAH, I pray thee, turn the counsel of Ahithophel into foolish-
ness. And it came to pass, that, when David was come to the top of
the ascent, where GOD was worshipped, behold, Hushai the Archite
came to meet him with his coat rent, and earth upon his head. And
David said unto him, If thou passest on with me, then thou wilt be a
burden unto me: but if thou return to the city, and say unto Absalom,
I will be thy servant, O king; as I have been thy father's servant in
time past, so will I now be thy servant; then wilt thou defeat for me
the counsel of Ahithophel."

2 Samuel 16:23-17:14, "And the counsel of Ahithophel, which he gave in those days, was as if a man inquired at the oracle of GOD: so was all the counsel of Ahithophel both with David and with Absalom. Moreover Ahithophel said unto Absalom, Let me now choose out twelve thousand men, and I will arise and pursue after David this night: and I will come upon him while he is weary and weak-handed, and will make him afraid; and all the people that are with him shall flee; and I will smite the king only; and I will bring back all the people unto thee: the man whom thou seekest is as if all returned: so all the people shall be in peace. And the saying pleased Absalom well, and all the elders of Israel. Then said Absalom, Call now Hushai the Archite also, and let us hear likewise what he saith. And when Hushai was come to Absalom, Absalom spake unto him, saying, Ahithophel hath spoken after this manner: shall we do after his saying? If not, speak you? And Hushai said unto Absalom, The counsel that Ahithophel hath given this time is not good. Hushai said moreover, Thou knowest thy father and his men, that they are mighty men, and they are chafed in their minds, as a bear robbed of her whelps in the field; and thy father is a man of war, and will not lodge with the people. Behold, he is hid now in some pit, or in some other place: and it will come to pass, when some of them are fallen at the first, that whosoever heareth it will say, There is a slaughter among the people that follow Absalom. And even he that is valiant, whose heart is as the heart of a lion, will utterly melt; for all Israel knoweth that thy father is a mighty man, and they that are with him are valiant men. But I counsel that all Israel be gathered together unto thee, from Dan even to Beer-sheba, as the sand that is by the sea for multitude; and that thou go to battle in thine own person. So shall we come upon him in some place where he shall be found, and we will light upon him as the dew falleth on the ground; and of him and of all the men that are with him we will not leave so much as one. Moreover, if he be gotten into a city, then shall all Israel bring ropes to that city, and we will draw it into the river, until there be not one small stone found there. And Absalom and all the men of Israel said, The counsel of Hushai the Archite is better than the counsel of Ahithophel. For JEHOVAH had ordained to defeat the good counsel of Ahithophel, to the intent that JEHOVAH might bring evil upon Absalom."

2 Samuel 17:21-23, "And it came to pass, after they were departed, that they came up out of the well, and went and told king David; and they said unto David, Arise ye, and pass quickly over the water; for thus hath Ahithophel counselled against you. Then David arose, and all the people that were with him, and they passed over the Jordan: by the morning light there lacked not one of them that was not gone over the Jordan. And when Ahithophel saw that his counsel was not followed, he saddled his ass, and arose, and gat him home, unto his city, and set his house in order, and hanged himself; and he died, and was buried in the sepulchre of his father."

1 Kings 10:23-11:13, "So king Solomon exceeded all the kings of the earth in riches and in wisdom. And all the earth sought the presence of Solomon, to hear his wisdom, which GOD had put in his heart. And they brought every man his tribute, vessels of silver, and vessels of gold, and raiment, and armor, and spices, horses, and mules, a rate year by year. And Solomon gathered together chariots and horsemen: and he had a thousand and four hundred chariots, and twelve thousand horsemen, that he bestowed in the chariot cities, and with the king at Jerusalem. And the king made silver to be in Jerusalem as stones, and cedars made he to be as the sycomore-trees that are in the lowland, for abundance. And the horses which Solomon had were brought out of Egypt; and the king's merchants received them in droves, each drove at a price. And a chariot came up and went out of Egypt for six hundred shekels of silver, and a horse for a hundred and fifty; and so for all the kings of the Hittites, and for the kings of Syria, did they bring them out by their means. Now king Solomon loved many foreign women, together with the daughter of Pharaoh, women of the Moabites, Ammonites, Edomites, Sidonians, and Hittites; of the nations concerning which JEHOVAH said unto the children of Israel, Ye shall not go among them, neither shall they come among you; for surely they will turn away your heart after their gods: Solomon clave unto these in love. And he had seven hundred wives, princesses, and three hundred concubines; and his wives turned away his heart. For it came to pass, when Solomon was old, that his wives turned away his heart after other gods; and his heart was not perfect with JEHOVAH his GOD, as was the heart of David his father. For Solomon went after Ashtoreth the goddess of the Sidonians, and after Milcom the abomination of the Ammonites. And Solomon did that which was evil in the sight of JEHOVAH, and went not fully after JEHOVAH, as did David his father. Then did Solomon build a high place for Chemosh the abomination of Moab, in the mount that is before Jerusalem, and for Molech the abomination of the children of Ammon. And so did he for all his foreign wives, who burnt incense and sacrificed unto their gods. And JEHOVAH was angry with Solomon, because his heart was turned away from JEHOVAH, the GOD of Israel, WHO had appeared unto him twice, and had commanded him concerning this thing, that he should not go after other gods: but he kept not that which JEHOVAH commanded. Wherefore JEHOVAH said unto Solomon, Forasmuch as this is done of thee, and thou hast not kept MY covenant and MY statutes, which I have commanded thee, I will surely rend the kingdom from thee, and will give it to thy servant. Notwithstanding in thy days I will not do it, for David thy father's sake: but I will rend it out of the hand of thy son. Howbeit I will not rend away all the kingdom; but I will give one tribe to thy son, for David MY servant's sake, and for Jerusalem's sake which I have chosen."

Ω

The purpose of wisdom is to provide a channel of peace and order. Wisdom builds bridges to respectable solutions. Ideally all will benefit as long as partners are willing to yield to resolutions. *The Holy Bible* tells a story of Solomon's perception from wisdom, and the well-known story of his wisdom concerning two women claiming the same son.

A

Ecclesiastes 9:13-18, "I have also seen wisdom under the sun on this wise, and it seemed great unto me: There was a little city, and few men within it; and there came a great king against it, and besieged it, and built great bulwarks against it. Now there was found in it a poor wise man, and he by his wisdom delivered the city; yet no man remembered that same poor man. Then said I, Wisdom is better than strength: nevertheless the poor man's wisdom is despised, and his words are not heard. The words of the wise heard in quiet are better than the cry of him that ruleth among fools. Wisdom is better than weapons of war; but one sinner destroyeth much good."

1 Kings 3:16-28, "Then there came two women that were harlots, unto the king, and stood before him. And the one woman said, Oh, my lord, I and this woman dwell in one house; and I was delivered of a child with her in the house. And it came to pass the third day after I was delivered, that this woman was delivered also; and we were together; there was no stranger with us in the house, save we two in the house. And this woman's child died in the night, because she lay upon it. And she arose at midnight, and took my son from beside me, while thy handmaid slept, and laid it in her bosom, and laid her dead child in my bosom. And when I rose in the morning to give my child suck, behold, it was dead; but when I had looked at it in the morning, behold, it was not my son, whom I did bear. And the other woman said, Nay; but the living is my son, and the dead is thy son. And this said, No; but the dead is thy son, and the living is my son. Thus they spake before the king. Then said the king, The one saith, This is my son that liveth, and thy son is the dead: and the other saith, Nay; but thy son is the dead, and my son is the living. And the king said, Fetch me a sword. And they brought a sword before the king. And the king said, Divide the living child in two, and give half to the one, and half to the other. Then spake the woman whose the living child was unto the king, for her heart yearned over her son, and she said, Oh, my lord, give her the living child, and in no wise slay it. But the other said, It shall be neither mine nor thine; divide it. Then the king answered and said, Give her the living child, and in no wise slay it: she is the mother thereof. And all Israel heard of the judgment which the king had judged; and they feared the king: for they saw that the wisdom of GOD was in him, to do justice."

Ω

The early Church used wisdom to resolve the rising issues of their time. They had to get organized, because JESUS did not give them step by step instructions. Their experience and debate based in scripture empowered by the HOLY SPIRIT were the tools they used to make rational policy for HIS Church.

A

Acts 6:1-7, "Now in these days, when the number of the disciples was multiplying, there arose a murmuring of the Grecian Jews against the Hebrews, because their widows were neglected in the daily ministration. And the twelve called the multitude of the disciples unto them, and said, It is not fit that we should forsake the WORD of GOD, and serve tables. Look ye out therefore, brethren, from among you seven men of good report, full of the SPIRIT and of wisdom, whom we may appoint over this business. But we will continue stedfastly in prayer, and in the ministry of the WORD. And the saying pleased the whole multitude: and they chose Stephen, a man full of faith and of the HOLY SPIRIT, and Philip, and Prochorus, and Nicanor, and Timon, and Parmenas, and Nicolaus a proselyte of Antioch; whom they set before the apostles: and when they had prayed, they laid their hands upon them. And the WORD of GOD increased; and the number of the disciples multiplied in Jerusalem exceedingly; and a great company of the priests were obedient to the faith."

Acts 15:5-21, "But there rose up certain of the sect of the Pharisees who believed, saying, It is needful to circumcise them, and to charge

134

them to keep the law of Moses. And the apostles and the elders were gathered together to consider of this matter. And when there had been much questioning, Peter rose up, and said unto them, Brethren, ye know that a good while ago GOD made choice among you, that by my mouth the Gentiles should hear the WORD of the gospel, and believe. And GOD, WHO knoweth the heart, bare them witness, giving them the HOLY SPIRIT, even as HE did unto us; and HE made no distinction between us and them, cleansing their hearts by faith. Now therefore why make ye trial of GOD, that ye should put a yoke upon the neck of the disciples which neither our fathers nor we were able to bear? But we believe that we shall be saved through the grace of the LORD JESUS, in like manner as they. And all the multitude kept silence; and they hearkened unto Barnabas and Paul rehearsing what signs and wonders GOD had wrought among the Gentiles through them. And after they had held their peace, James answered, saying, Brethren, hearken unto me: Symeon hath rehearsed how first GOD visited the Gentiles, to take out of them a people for HIS name. And to this agree the words of the prophets; as it is written, After these things I will return, And I will build again the tabernacle of David, which is fallen; And I will build again the ruins thereof, And I will set it up: That the residue of men may seek after the LORD, And all the Gentiles, upon whom MY name is called, Saith the LORD, WHO maketh these things known from of old. Wherefore my judgment is, that we trouble not them that from among the Gentiles turn to GOD; but that we write unto them, that they abstain from the pollutions of idols, and from fornication, and from what is strangled, and from blood. For Moses from generations of old hath in every city them that preach HIM, being read in the synagogues every sabbath."

1 Corinthians 14:26-33, "What is it then, brethren? When ye come together, each one hath a psalm, hath a teaching, hath a revelation, hath a tongue, hath an interpretation. Let all things be done unto edifying. If any man speaketh in a tongue, let it be by two, or at the most three, and that in turn; and let one interpret: but if there be no interpreter, let him keep silence in the church; and let him speak to himself, and to GOD. And let the prophets speak by two or three, and let

135

the others discern. But if a revelation be made to another sitting by, let the first keep silence. For ye all can prophesy one by one, that all may learn, and all may be exhorted; and the spirits of the prophets are subject to the prophets; for GOD is not a god of confusion, but of peace. As in all the churches of the saints,"

1 Corinthians 14:40, "But let all things be done decently and in order."

Ω

Understanding organizes thought into a workable plan regulated by the values of GOD through JESUS CHRIST. GOD has a plan. For every scenario that attempts to thwart HIS plan, HE has contingency plans to redirect events back to HIS narrative. HIS plan consists of the creation, restoration from the sin of Adam, the chosen people, the manifestation of CHRIST, the resurrection of CHRIST, and the eternal kingdom.

A

Genesis 2:16-17, "And JEHOVAH GOD commanded the man, saying, Of every tree of the garden thou mayest freely eat: but of the tree of the knowledge of good and evil, thou shalt not eat of it: for in the day that thou eatest thereof thou shalt surely die."

Genesis 3:1-6, "Now the serpent was more subtle than any beast of the field which JEHOVAH GOD had made. And he said unto the woman, Yea, hath GOD said, Ye shall not eat of any tree of the garden? And the woman said unto the serpent, Of the fruit of the trees of the garden we may eat: but of the fruit of the tree which is in the midst of the garden, GOD hath said, Ye shall not eat of it, neither shall ye touch it, lest ye die. And the serpent said unto the woman, Ye shall not surely die: for GOD doth know that in the day ye eat thereof, then your eyes shall be opened, and ye shall be as GOD, knowing good and evil. And when the woman saw that the tree was good for food, and that it was a delight to the eyes, and that the tree was to be desired to make one wise, she took of the fruit thereof, and did eat; and she gave also unto her husband with her, and he did eat."

Genesis 17:1-8, "And when Abram was ninety years old and nine, JEHOVAH appeared to Abram, and said unto him, I am GOD ALMIGHTY; walk before ME, and be thou perfect. And I will make MY covenant between ME and thee, and will multiply thee exceedingly. And Abram fell on his face: and GOD talked with him, saying, As for ME, behold, MY covenant is with thee, and thou shalt be the father of a multitude of nations. Neither shall thy name any more be called Abram, but thy name shall be Abraham; for the father of a multitude of nations have I made thee. And I will make thee exceeding fruitful, and I will make nations of thee, and kings shall come out of thee. And I will establish MY covenant between ME and thee and thy seed after thee throughout their generations for an everlasting covenant, to be a GOD unto thee and to thy seed after thee. And I will give unto thee, and to thy SEED after thee, the land of thy sojournings, all the land of Canaan, for an everlasting possession; and I will be their GOD."

Galatians 3:16, "Now to Abraham were the promises spoken, and to his SEED. HE saith not, And to seeds, as of many; but as of ONE, And to thy SEED, which is CHRIST."

Genesis 21:1-7, "And JEHOVAH visited Sarah as HE had said, and JEHOVAH did unto Sarah as HE had spoken. And Sarah conceived, and bare Abraham a son in his old age, at the set time of which GOD had spoken to him. And Abraham called the name of his son that was born unto him, whom Sarah bare to him, Isaac. And Abraham circumcised his son Isaac when he was eight days old, as GOD had commanded him. And Abraham was a hundred years old, when his son Isaac was born unto him. And Sarah said, GOD hath made me to laugh. Every one that heareth will laugh with me. And she said, Who would have said unto Abraham, that Sarah should give children suck? For I have borne him a son in his old age."

Exodus 1:8-16, "Now there arose a new king over Egypt, who knew not Joseph. And he said unto his people, Behold, the people of the children of Israel are more and mightier than we: come, let us deal wisely with them, lest they multiply, and it come to pass, that, when there falleth out any war, they also join themselves unto our enemies, and fight against us, and get them up out of the land. Therefore they did set over them taskmasters to afflict them with their burdens. And they built for Pharaoh store-cities, Pithom and Raamses. But the more they afflicted them, the more they multiplied and the more they spread abroad. And they were grieved because of the children of Israel. And the Egyptians made the children of Israel to serve with rigor: and they made their lives bitter with hard service, in mortar and in brick, and in all manner of service in the field, all their service, wherein they made them serve with rigor. And the king of Egypt spake to the Hebrew midwives, of whom the name of the one was Shiphrah, and the name of the other Puah: and he said, When ye do the office of a midwife to the Hebrew women, and see them upon the birth-stool; if it be a son, then ye shall kill him; but if it be a daughter, then she shall live."

Matthew 2:16, "Then Herod, when he saw that he was mocked of the Wise-men, was exceeding wroth, and sent forth, and slew all the male children that were in Bethlehem, and in all the borders thereof, from two years old and under, according to the time which he had exactly learned of the Wise-men."

Luke 1:26-33, "Now in the sixth month the angel Gabriel was sent from GOD unto a city of Galilee, named Nazareth, to a virgin betrothed to a man whose name was Joseph, of the house of David; and the virgin's name was Mary. And he came in unto her, and said, Hail, thou that art highly favored, the LORD is with thee. But she was greatly troubled at the saying, and cast in her mind what manner of salutation this might be. And the angel said unto her, Fear not, Mary:

138

for thou hast found favor with GOD. And behold, thou shalt conceive in thy womb, and bring forth a SON, and shalt call HIS name JESUS. HE shall be great, and shall be called the SON of the MOST HIGH: and the LORD GOD shall give unto HIM the throne of HIS father David: and HE shall reign over the house of Jacob for ever; and of HIS kingdom there shall be no end."

Ω

I crucified my LORD, and simultaneously I am crucified with HIM. JESUS forgives me, conquers death, and opens the door of opportunity for me. GOD's plan has been about paving an avenue for saving me.

A

Mark 15:25-37, "And it was the third hour, and they crucified HIM. And the superscription of HIS accusation was written over, THE KING OF THE JEWS. And with HIM they crucify two robbers; one on HIS right hand, and one on HIS left. And the scripture was fulfilled, which saith, And HE was reckoned with transgressors. And they that passed by railed on HIM, wagging their heads, and saying, Ha! THOU that destroyest the temple, and buildest it in three days, save THYSELF, and come down from the cross. In like manner also the chief priests mocking HIM among themselves with the scribes said, HE saved others; HIMSELF HE cannot save. Let the CHRIST, the KING of Israel, now come down from the cross, that we may see and believe. And they that were crucified with HIM reproached HIM. And when the sixth hour was come, there was darkness over the whole land until the ninth hour. And at the ninth hour JESUS cried with a loud voice, Eloi, Eloi, lama sabachthani? which is, being interpreted, MY GOD, MY GOD, why hast thou forsaken ME? And some of them that stood by, when they heard it, said, Behold, HE calleth Elijah. And one ran, and filling a sponge full of vinegar, put it on a reed, and gave HIM to drink, saying, Let be; let us see whether

Elijah cometh to take HIM down. And JESUS uttered a loud voice, and gave up the ghost."

Luke 23:34, "And JESUS said, FATHER, forgive them; for they know not what they do. And parting HIS garments among them, they cast lots."

John 20:11-18, "But Mary was standing without at the tomb weeping: so, as she wept, she stooped and looked into the tomb; and she beholdeth two angels in white sitting, one at the head, and one at the feet, where the body of JESUS had lain. And they say unto her, Woman, why weepest thou? She saith unto them, Because they have taken away my LORD, and I know not where they have laid HIM. When she had thus said, she turned herself back, and beholdeth JESUS standing, and knew not that it was JESUS. JESUS saith unto her, Woman, why weepest thou? WHOM seekest thou? She, supposing HIM to be the gardener, saith unto HIM, SIR, if THOU hast borne HIM hence, tell me where thou hast laid HIM, and I will take HIM away. JESUS saith unto her, Mary. She turneth herself, and saith unto HIM in Hebrew, RABBONI; which is to say, TEACHER. JESUS saith to her, Touch ME not; for I am not yet ascended unto the FATHER: but go unto MY brethren, and say to them, I ascend unto MY FATHER and your FATHER, and MY GOD and your GOD. Mary Magdalene cometh and telleth the disciples, I have seen the LORD; and that HE had said these things unto her."

Luke 24:36-49, "And as they (the disciples) spake these things, HE (JESUS) HIMSELF stood in the midst of them, and saith unto them, Peace be unto you. But they were terrified and affrighted, and supposed that they beheld a spirit. And HE said unto them, Why are ye troubled? and wherefore do questionings arise in your heart? See MY hands and MY feet, that it is I MYSELF: handle ME, and see; for a spirit hath not flesh and bones, as ye behold ME having. And when HE had said this, HE showed them HIS hands and HIS feet. And while they still disbelieved for joy, and wondered, HE said unto them, Have ye here anything to eat? And they gave HIM a piece of a broiled fish. And HE took it, and ate before them. And HE said unto them, These are MY WORDS which I spake unto you, while I was yet with you, that all things must needs be fulfilled, which are written in the law of Moses, and the prophets, and the psalms, concerning ME. Then opened HE their mind, that they might understand the scriptures; and HE said unto them, Thus it is written, that the CHRIST should suffer, and rise again from the dead the third day; and that repentance and remission of sins should be preached in HIS name unto all the nations, beginning from Jerusalem. Ye are witnesses of these things. And behold, I send forth the promise of MY FATHER upon you: but tarry ye in the city, until ye be clothed with power from on high."

Revelation 21:10-23, "And he (an angel) carried me (the Apostle John) away in the SPIRIT to a mountain great and high, and showed me the holy city Jerusalem, coming down out of heaven from GOD, having the glory of GOD: her light was like unto a stone most precious, as it were a jasper stone, clear as crystal: having a wall great and high; having twelve gates, and at the gates twelve angels; and names written thereon, which are the names of the twelve tribes of the children of Israel: on the east were three gates; and on the north three gates; and on the south three gates; and on the west three gates. And the wall of the city had twelve foundations, and on them twelve names of the twelve apostles of the LAMB. And he that spake with me had for a measure a golden reed to measure the city, and the gates thereof, and the wall thereof. And the city lieth foursquare, and the length thereof is as great as the breadth: and he measured the city with the reed, twelve thousand furlongs: the length and the breadth and the height thereof are equal. And he measured the wall thereof, a hundred and forty and four cubits, according to the measure of a man, that is, of an angel. And the building of the wall thereof was jasper: and the city was pure gold, like unto pure glass. The foundations of the wall of the city were adorned with all manner of precious stones. The first foundation was jasper; the second, sapphire; the third, chalcedony; the fourth, emerald; the fifth, sardonyx; the sixth, sardius; the seventh, chrysolite; the eighth, beryl; the ninth, topaz; the tenth, chryso-prase; the eleventh, jacinth; the twelfth, amethyst. And the twelve gates were twelve pearls; each one of the several gates was of one pearl: and the street of the city was pure gold, as it were transparent glass. And I saw no temple therein: for the LORD GOD the ALMIGHTY, and the LAMB, are the temple thereof. And the city hath no need of the sun, neither of the moon, to shine upon it: for the glory of GOD did lighten it, and the lamp thereof is the LAMB."

Ω

GOD values me as a part of HIS plan. To create this universe and the intricacies of my life interwoven within that plan is inconceivable to me. HE desires fellowship, and all HIS wisdom and works reflect it.

Summary

Chapter 11

I am seeking GOD, WHO wants to be found, and I know this because HE has left evidence in HIS WORD. Life, humility, righteousness, patience, faithfulness, fellowship, and wisdom are the facets of GOD's identity, and all who respond in like manner has GOD's attention. My response in HIS identity ignites HIS response to my situation. HE is ready to act for me, but I must be willing to be like HIM.

A

Job 36:7, "HE withdraweth not HIS eyes from the righteous: But with kings upon the throne HE setteth them for ever, and they are exalted."

Psalms 34:15, "The eyes of JEHOVAH are toward the righteous, And HIS ears are open unto their cry."

1 Peter 3:12, "For the eyes of the LORD are upon the righteous, And HIS ears unto their supplication: But the face of the LORD is upon them that do evil."

Ω

It is possible to find GOD, but not know HIS numinous ways. Who HE acts upon, and what causes HIM to act are known. How HE acts, when HE acts, and where HE acts are unknown. As I focus on loving HIM, I become the "who" HE acts upon, because I know what causes HIM to act towards my benefit. HIS identity acting through my person is to HIS glory.

A

Galatians 2:20, "I have been crucified with CHRIST; and it is no longer I that live, but CHRIST living in me: and that life which I now live in the flesh I live in faith, the faith which is in the SON of GOD, WHO loved me, and gave HIMSELF up for me."

Ω

I am an expression of CHRIST. Being a Christian, is not about dying, and going to an infallible place. It is about living, for today is the day of salvation. When I accept JESUS in my heart, eternity begins. Eternity is not a stop and start, it is a continuation of my life into the infinite. For a Christian, it is like getting a promotion to a higher position on the job as I continue with the company except my work is recognized by the KING of kings and LORD of lords, and HE puts me in the position of HIS choosing.

A

Matthew 22:23-32, "On that day there came to HIM (JESUS) Sadducees, they that say that there is no resurrection: and they asked HIM, saying, TEACHER, Moses said, If a man die, having no children, his brother shall marry his wife, and raise up seed unto his brother. Now there were with us seven brethren: and the first married and deceased, and having no seed left his wife unto his brother; in like manner the second also, and the third, unto the seventh. And after them all, the woman died. In the resurrection therefore whose wife shall she be of the seven? for they all had her. But JESUS answered and said unto them, Ye do err, not knowing the scriptures, nor the power of GOD. For in the resurrection they neither marry, nor are given in marriage, but are as angels in heaven. But as touching the resurrection of the dead, have ye not read that which was spoken unto you by GOD, saying, I am the GOD of Abraham, and the GOD of Isaac, and the GOD of Jacob? GOD is not the GOD of the dead, but of the living."

Isaiah 49:8-9, "Thus saith JEHOVAH, In an acceptable time have I answered thee, and in a day of salvation have I helped thee; and I will preserve thee, and give thee for a covenant of the people, to raise up the land, to make them inherit the desolate heritages: saying to them that are bound, Go forth; to them that are in darkness, Show yourselves. They shall feed in the ways, and on all bare heights shall be their pasture."

2 Corinthians 6:2, "(for HE (GOD) saith, At an acceptable time I hearkened unto thee, And in a day of salvation did I succor thee: behold, now is the acceptable time; behold, now is the day of salvation):"

Ω

GOD desires me to be a steward of HIS values. HE appreciates my practical and intellectual pursuits of the weightier matters that are important to HIM. HE is not one to shutter from my evaluation of HIM, and in fact, and HE welcomes the invitation of reasoning. HE rarely answers by fire with clamorous thundering, so I must recognize when the answer comes from HIS still small voice.

A

Isaiah 1:18-20, "Come now, and let us reason together, saith JEHOVAH: though your sins be as scarlet, they shall be as white as snow; though they be red like crimson, they shall be as wool. If ye be willing and obedient, ye shall eat the good of the land: but if ye refuse and rebel, ye shall be devoured with the sword; for the mouth of JEHOVAH hath spoken it."

Isaiah 43:23-26, "Thou (the children of Israel) hast not brought ME (GOD) of thy sheep for burnt-offerings; neither hast thou honored ME with thy sacrifices. I have not burdened thee with offerings, nor wearied thee with frankincense. Thou hast bought ME no sweet cane

145

with money, neither hast thou filled ME with the fat of thy sacrifices; but thou hast burdened ME with thy sins, thou hast wearied ME with thine iniquities. I, even I, am HE that blotteth out thy transgressions for MINE own sake; and I will not remember thy sins. Put ME in remembrance; let us plead together: set thou forth thy cause, that thou mayest be justified."

1 Kings 19:1-18, "And Ahab told Jezebel all that Elijah had done, and withal how he had slain all the prophets with the sword. Then Jezebel send a messenger unto Elijah, saying, So let the gods do to me, and more also, if I make not thy life as the life of one of them by to-morrow about this time. And when he saw that, he arose, and went for his life, and came to Beer-sheba, which belongeth to Judah, and left his servant there. But he himself went a day's journey into the wilderness, and came and sat down under a juniper-tree: and he requested for himself that he might die, and said, It is enough; now, O JEHOVAH, take away my life; for I am not better than my fathers. And he lay down and slept under a juniper-tree; and, behold, an angel touched him, and said unto him, Arise and eat. And he looked, and, behold, there was at his head a cake baken on the coals, and a cruse of water. And he did eat and drink, and laid him down again. And the angel of JEHOVAH came again the second time, and touched him, and said, Arise and eat, because the journey is too great for thee. And he arose, and did eat and drink, and went in the strength of that food forty days and forty nights unto Horeb the mount of GOD. And he came thither unto a cave, and lodged there; and, behold, the WORD of JEHOVAH came to him, and HE said unto him, What doest thou here, Elijah? And he said, I have been very jealous for JEHOVAH, the GOD of hosts; for the children of Israel have forsaken THY covenant, thrown down THINE altars, and slain THY prophets with the sword: and I, even I only, am left; and they seek my life, to take it away. And HE said, Go forth, and stand upon the mount before JEHOVAH. And, behold, JEHOVAH passed by, and a great and strong wind rent the mountains, and brake in pieces the rocks before JEHOVAH; but JEHOVAH was not in the wind: and after the wind an earthquake; but JEHOVAH was not in the earthquake: and after

146

the earthquake a fire; but JEHOVAH was not in the fire: and after the fire a still small voice. And it was so, when Elijah heard it, that he wrapped his face in his mantle, and went out, and stood in the entrance of the cave. And, behold, there came a voice unto him, and said, What doest thou here, Elijah? And he said, I have been very jealous for JEHOVAH, the GOD of hosts; for the children of Israel have forsaken THY covenant, thrown down THINE altars, and slain THY prophets with the sword; and I, even I only, am left; and they seek my life, to take it away. And JEHOVAH said unto him, Go, return on thy way to the wilderness of Damascus: and when thou comest, thou shalt anoint Hazael to be king over Syria; and Jehu the son of Nimshi shalt thou anoint to be king over Israel; and Elisha the son of Shaphat of Abel-meholah shalt thou anoint to be prophet in thy room. And it shall come to pass, that him that escapeth from the sword of Hazael shall Jehu slay; and him that escapeth from the sword of Jehu shall Elisha slay. Yet will I leave ME seven thousand in Israel, all the knees which have not bowed unto Baal, and every mouth which hath not kissed him."

John 10:1-6, "Verily, verily, I (JESUS) say unto you, He that entereth not by the door into the fold of the sheep, but climbeth up some other way, the same is a thief and a robber. But HE that entereth in by the door is the SHEPHERD of the sheep. To HIM the porter openeth; and the sheep hear HIS voice: and HE calleth HIS own sheep by name, and leadeth them out. When HE hath put forth all HIS own, HE goeth before them, and the sheep follow HIM: for they know HIS voice. And a stranger will they not follow, but will flee from him: for they know not the voice of strangers. This parable spake JESUS unto them: but they understood not what things they were which HE spake unto them."

Ω

In a dialogue with a coworker about believing in GOD, my colleague expressed how GOD did not grant a prayer request for a

147

loved one to live. Without thought, I began to slowly and softly speak. "You can't do that to HIM. HE doesn't work on your terms. I remember when my Dad had just had both legs amputated. My Mom was broken and crying as she told me over the phone that he was not in his right mind, and that he didn't know who she was.

Driving to Little Rock, it seemed like I prayed all the way there. I said, "GOD, I know all things are possible to YOU. I know YOU can give him his legs back. I know YOU can restore him. I just don't know if YOU will. If YOU don't give me anything else, I need his mind."" Looking back, as I prayed, I was negotiating each possibly with the ALMIGHTY.

"When I arrived in the hospital room, my Mom and I held each other, but my Dad was physically present, and not in his right mind. My Dad called to people from his childhood, who had long passed. The helplessness of seeing my Dad like that gripped me. I sat in a chair uttering, "My GOD. My GOD." In the middle of my grief, I thought, "Music." My mind began racing as I gathered thoughts about how do I get my hands on some music, which radio station, and what artists.

Fortunately, I had my smartphone, "Pandora," as my thoughts began to race, and then I remembered how much he liked, "Motown," in his youth. The first song that played, he started singing. By the third song, all of us were talking, and my Mom and I were overflowing with joy. My Dad was sing to my Mom, and bopping on the hospital bed. All that happened in less than an hour after I walked through the door of his hospital room.

From that day, I had my Dad for two more years in his right mind before he passed. "Am I supposed to be angry with GOD because my Dad's legs didn't come back or because he passed? While in his wheelchair, in those two years, we went fishing a couple of times, my Mom and Dad vacationed in Chicago to spend time with my brother, sister-in-law, and their two daughters (my parent's granddaughters), and my sister and brother-in-law took my parents on a tour of the Bass Pro Shop at the Memphis Pyramid. At church, I watched my Dad roll in his wheelchair to the altar, and the pastor handed him the microphone. He lifted his arms, and proclaimed, "GOD is good!" No... GOD exceeded my expectations."

A

Jeremiah 29:8-14, "For thus saith JEHOVAH of hosts, the GOD of Israel: Let not your prophets that are in the midst of you, and your diviners, deceive you; neither hearken ye to your dreams which ye cause to be dreamed. For they prophesy falsely unto you in MY name: I have not sent them, saith JEHOVAH. For thus saith JEHOVAH, After seventy years are accomplished for Babylon, I will visit you, and perform MY good WORD toward you, in causing you to return to this place. For I know the thoughts that I think toward you, saith JEHOVAH, thoughts of peace, and not of evil, to give you hope in your latter end. And ye shall call upon ME, and ye shall go and pray unto ME, and I will hearken unto you. And ye shall seek ME, and find ME, when ye shall search for ME with all your heart. And I will be found of you, saith JEHOVAH, and I will turn again your captivity, and I will gather you from all the nations, and from all the places wither I have driven you, saith JEHOVAH; and I will bring you again unto the place whence I caused you to be carried away captive."

Ω

GOD is watching.

149

About the Author

The Holy Bible states that GOD takes the foolish things of this world to confound the wise. I have no degrees of scholarly merit, bi-racial, and my last name is Gross. Sometimes I have to laugh at GOD's humor. Living in Bartlett, Tennessee, a suburb of Memphis, I make my rounds as a delivery driver. My days are spent meeting wonderful people on a regular basis.

www.ingramcontent.com/pod-product-compliance
Lightning Source LLC
Chambersburg PA
CBHW061726020426
42331CB00006B/1121